CAREER CHOICES

A Guide for Teens and Young Adults:
Who Am I?
What Do I Want?
How Do I Get It?

Written by Mindy Bingham and Sandy Stryker
Edited by Robert F. Shafer

Illustrated by Itoko Maeno, Janice Blair, and Diana Lackner

Able Publishing, Santa Barbara

To Bob

   Thanks for helping me find me again.

To Bill

   With love and gratitude for your patience and support.

Published by Able Publishing
3463 State Street, Suite 219A
Santa Barbara, CA 93105.
(805) 967-8015   FAX (805) 967-7741

Manufactured in the United States of America

Copies of this book are available in better bookstores or may be ordered by sending $22.95 ppd to Career Choices, Able Publishing, 3463 State Street, Suite 219A, Santa Barbara, CA 93105, U.S.A. (California residents add sales tax.)

An Instructor's and Counselor's Manual is available for $21.95 ppd along with a workbook for $5.95 ppd at the above address.

10 9 8 7 6 5 4 3

We have taken the privilege of substituting certain words in the quotations cited here ("person" instead of "man," "people" instead of "men") to make them more inclusive, with the certainty that, had they been said today, this is how they would have been stated.

This book belongs to _____

Started on _____

Completed on _____

I dedicate this work to _____

Know thyself
Socrates

CONTENTS

The assignment was puzzling in light of the fact that they were supposed to start a unit on career planning today. But Mr. Ziegfeld refused to elaborate. "Bring me something that flies," he'd said. As the students began to drift into the classroom, it was clear that they had interpreted the assignment in a variety of ways.

Beautifully decorated kites mingled with bunches of balloons. Model planes ran the gamut from Wilbur and Orville Wright's first craft to the latest supersonic jets. There were helicopters and spaceships, gliders and seaplanes. Working models of a blimp and a hot air balloon hovered near the ceiling. Several superheroes were represented, with Superman and Wonder Woman apparently the favorites. Someone dressed like Charles Lindbergh chatted with an Amelia Earheart look-alike. Chuck Yeager, Sally Ride, and John Glenn impersonators joined the group. A pet parakeet's song was drowned out by the coos from a box of pigeons.

Finally, Mr. Ziegfeld called the class to order. Students took their seats, anxious to learn what this was all about. "Okay," he said. "Let's talk about career planning."

"Wait a minute," said Superman. "Aren't you going to explain the assignment? What does all this flying business have to do with choosing a career?"

Oh, that," Mr. Ziegfeld replied. "You'd probably figure it out soon enough. But I guess I can fill you in now. It's really quite simple. Deciding what to do with your life is a lot like learning to fly. I just wanted you to see that there are lots of ways to do it. Take a look around the room and hold on to this image.

"What's right for Charles Lindbergh will probably not suit Sally Ride. Yet both of them are heroes. Some people take direct flights. Others stop at points of interest along the way. The pace of the journey is an individual matter as well. That's why it's important to know who you are and what you want.

"You won't necessarily choose your life's career in this class. But you will learn a process that you can use again and again, as you adjust to the future and keep making plans. Once you learn this, you'll be able to proceed more easily, no matter what you decide to do.

"Now, let's get started. Up and away!"

CHAPTER ONE

Envisioning Your Future

How do you define success?

Personal success is simply the fulfillment
of what makes you happiest.
—Anonymous

Vision is the art of seeing the invisible.
—Jonathan Swift

Section One:
WHO AM I?

MICHAEL GETS THE MAGIC JUMPING BEANS

One day, Michael Jordan noticed an old woman attempting to cross the street against heavy traffic. He took the woman's arm and guided her safely to the other side. "Thank you, young man," she said in a thin, wobbly voice. "I want to give you something for your trouble." With that, she reached into her pocket and pulled out three small, round objects that looked as though they'd been kept there for years. "What are these?" Michael asked. "These are my magic jumping beans," she said. "Swallow them with a glass of Dr. Pepper at three o'clock on a Friday afternoon, and they will make you a great basketball star. You will be able to jump higher and stay in the air longer than any other player. I've been saving the beans for myself, but it's beginning to look as though I won't live long enough to see professional women's basketball succeed. Here, do as I tell you." "Okay," Michael said enthusiastically.

SALLY WINS THE ASTRO-LOTTERY

Sally Ride was working a crossword puzzle and watching "Jeopardy" one evening when her phone rang. "Congratulations," said the voice on the line, "your name has just been picked from 20 million entries to be the first woman astronaut in America! What do you think of that?" "Gee, it sounds great," said Sally. "Yes, Sally," the voice continued, "you are our lucky winner. You'll be flown as our guest to the luxury astronaut training center in beautiful Houston, Texas, where you will learn space secrets and survival techniques from the experts. Then it'll be off to sunny Cape Canaveral, where you'll blast off into space as millions of people around the world watch and cheer. Your prize also includes the regulation space suit, the freeze-dried gourmet dinners, and assurance that your name will go down in history! What do you say to that, Sally Ride?" "Wow," said Sally.

OPRAH GETS DISCOVERED

Oprah Winfrey got on a downtown bus to go shopping one Saturday. The bus was crowded, and she accidentally stepped on the foot of a man sitting near the front. "Excuse me," she said. The man looked at her. "Would you say that again," he asked. "Excuse me?" said Oprah. "That's it! People, this is the one!" the man exclaimed. "This is our star!" As he made his announcement, a dozen people jumped up from seats further back in the bus. A camera crew descended on Oprah with microphones and glaring lights. Someone from make-up began highlighting her cheekbones. A hairdresser told Oprah she'd be stunning as a blond. "Wait a minute," Oprah demanded. "What's this all about?" "You're going to be the star of our new talk show," the first man told her. "You'll have your own production company. And you'll make some movies, too. The job pays about 25 million dollars a year. How does that sound?" "Sounds good to me," said Oprah.

GEORGE FINDS A JOB

One day, while vacationing in Washington, D.C., George Bush saw a sign in the White House window. "Help Wanted," it read. Since he was between jobs at the time, George decided to check it out. "We're looking for the next President of the United States," the woman in the office told him. "You have to be an American citizen, and you must be over 35 years of age." "That's me," said George. "Do I get the job?" "I don't see why not," the woman said. "Of course, you'll have to re-locate. Would you mind living in the White House?" "Well, I don't know. Could I think about it for a day or two and get back to you?" "Sure. Take your time. No pressure."

11

VISION + ENERGY = SUCCESS

You can safely assume that there is not one kernel of truth in any of the preceding stories. Successful people do not depend on luck or magic to get what they want. Nor do they let others make their career choices for them. Most people who are successful in their work don't just *find* a job. They *make* one. They have a *vision* of what they would like to do, how they would like to use their minds, talents, and interests. And they have the *energy* to make their dreams come true. They believe in their vision.

Vision and energy (or action) are the two most important elements in getting what you want from life. Your vision of what you'd like to do or be, or how you'd like to live, will help you know when you've succeeded. A goal is like a compass that will help keep you on track. And your energy or actions will take you, step by step, to the realization of your vision.

It is essential to have *both* elements. Vision without action is just daydreaming. Alone, it won't get you anywhere. Undirected action is equally useless. It leads only to exhaustion and frustration. Together, though, they are a dynamic duo. And they can work for you, no matter what your goal. (Not everyone can — or wants to — be a superstar. You need to have your own definition of success. More on that later in this chapter.)

What do you think are the *real* stories behind the successful people we talked about on the preceding pages? For the following exercises, write a statement that you feel might reflect his or her vision. Then list some actions they may have taken to realize their goal. Michael Jordan's chart, for example, might look something like this:

Michael Jordan

Vision: To be a top professional basketball player, someone who adds something new to the game.

Actions in school: Throughout grade school, high school, and college, practice, practice, practice; seek out good coaching; watch and analyze top players; keep up grades in order to be eligible for team play; stay healthy.

Actions at work: As a pro, practice, practice, practice; maintain health.

Complete charts for the following individuals.

Sally Ride

Vision: _____

Actions in school: _____

Actions at work: _____

Oprah Winfrey

Vision: _____

Actions in school: _____

Actions at work: _____

George Bush

Vision: _____

Actions in school: _____

Actions at work: _____

Envisioning Your Future

What about you? Do you have a vision for your own future? You need to begin imagining one if you don't. It's an important first step. Once you have a vision, you start expecting to realize it. What you *expect* for yourself tends to become what you *get*. So imagine a *positive* future for yourself.

Sit quietly, close your eyes, and imagine your ideal career. What kind of setting are you in? What tasks are you performing? Are you working alone or with others? How do you feel about yourself? Describe your vision in as much detail as possible.

_____

_____

_____

_____

_____

_____

_____

_____

_____

Was that a difficult exercise for you? Don't worry about it if it was. The rest of this book is designed to help you begin to clarify who you are, what you want, and what you need to do to get it. So keep reading!

Why People Work

People work for many reasons, but, basically, they work to bring personal meaning and satisfaction to themselves as well as benefits to society. All human beings have a need to work, to do, and to become someone through that process. According to Kenneth B. Hoyt, known as 'the father of career education', we work to "discover both *who* we are and *why* we are."

Of course, people also work for survival. In early history, that meant — literally — bringing home the bacon (or the woolly mammoth), gathering fruits and grains, and finding shelter from the elements. Today the transaction is less direct. People work for *money*, which they use to fulfill the same basic needs. But then, you probably already knew that. You may be less aware, however, of some *of the other* reasons people go to work each day. The following come from Dr. Jay B. Rohrlich's book, *Work and Love: the crucial balance.*

People work to define themselves. Ask most people who they are, and they will respond with their occupation: "I'm a mail carrier," "I'm a sales representative," "I'm a teacher," and so on. It may be just as accurate to say "I'm an emotional person" or "I'm very creative." But, somehow, statements like these seem more ambiguous. They provide less concrete information. Being able to provide a job title or a list of accomplishments makes us feel more *real* to ourselves and others.

People work to have a sense of security. Many people find it difficult to get all the love or approval they need from their relationships with friends and family. For them, work can be a constant source of security and pleasure. They may not know what kind of mood they will find their spouse in on any given night. But they can be fairly certain that their work will be the same.

People work for self-respect, or to feel competent and powerful. It isn't always easy to feel powerful in the world. Some people will always be more powerful than you are. Discrimination based on sex or race is real and robs its victims of the feeling that they can direct the course of their lives. But doing a particular job well gives a worker a sense of control and responsibility that adds greatly to his or her self-respect.

People work to conquer time. We are aware from an early age that our time on earth is limited. The days that pass simply vanish. One way we can "conquer" time is to fill each day with achievements or accomplishments. Over time, these experiences become a real and lasting part of what we see ourselves to be.

People work to measure their self-worth. Working is one way of "keeping score," of seeing how we stack up in comparison to others. Who is the most accomplished? Who got the award or promotion? Who earned the respect of the group? Who makes the most money? These are all ways we use to measure our self-worth. We feel better about ourselves when we succeed at a *difficult* task than we do when we accomplish something easy. We also tend to place importance on public recognition: the more lives you touch, the longer you may be remembered.

In the long run, though, true job satisfaction comes only from inside. You are the final judge of your own achievement. Whether you make a fortune, or just a living, is less important than knowing that you made a contribution, and that you did your job well.

Everybody Works

Whether you currently earn money from a job or not, you are a worker. You are probably a student. Chances are, you do chores at home. Perhaps you are an athlete or a musician, a computer whiz or a video fanatic, a cook or a gardener. For the purpose of this exercise, consider all your studies, tasks, and hobbies as work.

Think about a typical "working day," one in which you spent time on most of your "jobs." List the tasks and activities you performed below. Make your list as complete as you can.

_____

_____

Based on that list, how would you define your jobs? Write your titles on the following lines.

I am a _____

_____

_____

What would be your accomplishments at the end of the day (an English paper, a clean room, a solved problem, and so on)? List them below.

_____

_____

_____

Which accomplishments are most satisfying? _____

_____

How do they make you feel about yourself? _____

_____

Do your feelings relate to any of the reasons people work listed on the previous page? Which ones?

_____

_____

Defining Success

According to the dictionary, success is "the achievement of something desired, planned, or attempted." Since your desires and plans are very personal and are not exactly like anyone else's, you will need to define success for yourself.

This is not an easy thing to do in our society. Success is often equated with wealth and fame, luxurious homes, and fancy cars. These outward displays may *look like* success to others, but they do not make those who possess them *feel* successful. The feeling of success comes only when *you achieve* what is *most important to you*. True success is a personal feeling, not a public display.

What does success mean to you? What would make you feel that you are a successful human being? In addition to thinking about what you do, contemplate the type of person you want to be.

Other people have made their opinions known as well. We've listed some of them below. Do any of them match your definition? Indicate whether you strongly agree, agree, are not sure, disagree, or strongly disagree with each statement.

	Strongly Agree	Agree	Not Sure	Disagree	Strongly Disagree
Money, achievement, fame and success are important, but they are bought too dearly when acquired at the cost of health. — Anonymous					
It's great to be great, but it's better to be human. — Will Rogers					
Nothing succeeds like excess. — Oscar Wilde					
Success is a journey, not a destination. — Ben Sweetland					
The fastest way to succeed is to look as if you're playing by other people's rules, while quietly playing by your own. — Michael Korda					
She could not separate success from peace of mind. The two must go together . . . — Daphne Du Maurier, *Mary Anne*					
All of us are born for a reason, but all of us don't discover why. Success in life has nothing to do with what you gain in life or accomplish for yourself. It's what you do for others. — Danny Thomas					
I've never sought success in order to get fame and money; it's the talent and the passion that count in success. — Ingrid Bergman					

	Stongly Agree	Agree	Not Sure	Disagree	Strongly Disagree
The two leading recipes for success are building a better mousetrap and finding a bigger loophole. — Edgar A. Shoaff					
Success is something to enjoy — to flaunt! Otherwise, why work so hard to get it? — Isobel Lennart, *Funny Girl*					
Success is knowing what your values are and living in a way consistent with your values. — Danny Cox					
Success can only be measured in terms of distance traveled... — Mavis Gallant					
If at first you don't succeed, you are running about average. — M. H. Anderson					
I think success has no rules, but you can learn a great deal from failure. — Jean Kerr, *Mary, Mary*					
Success can make you go one of two ways. It can make you a *prima donna,* or it can smooth the edges, take away the insecurities, let the nice things come out. — Barbara Walters					
Six essential qualities that are the key to success: Sincerity, personal integrity, humility, courtesy, wisdom, charity. — Dr. William Menninger					
The people who try to do something and fail are infinitely better than those who try to do nothing and succeed. — Lloyd Jones					
The wealthy man is the man who is much, not the one who has much. — Karl Marx					
Winning isn't everything — it's the only thing. — Vince Lombardi					
Only those who dare to fail greatly can ever achieve greatly. — Robert F. Kennedy					
If at first you don't succeed, try, try again. Then give up. There's no use being a fool about it. — W. C. Fields					
I'm opposed to millionaires, but it would be dangerous to offer me the position. — Mark Twain					

Making Career Choices

Later in the book, you will learn a technique that will help you make good decisions in most situations. For now, though, as you begin making choices about your future career, try to be aware of the decision-making patterns you use most often. Some of them work better than others. Some of them don't work at all. Do you recognize yourself in any of the following stories?

ERIC has a tendency toward wishful thinking. He concentrates on the outcome that seems most attractive to him. But he pays little attention to the risks involved, or the probability of his wish coming true. Eric has decided to be a professional tennis player, even though he's not willing to practice. Last spring he was cut from the school's tennis team.

LOUISA is an escape artist. She takes pride in determining the worst thing that could happen in any situation. And, even when there is little chance of that outcome, she chooses a safe alternative. Although Louisa is a straight A student in math, she is afraid she wouldn't do as well in that subject in college. She'd like to be an engineer, but she's decided to major in elementary education.

MAGGIE likes to play it safe. She knows she could be successful as an insurance agent, so she plans to follow that course. Really, though, she'd rather be a politician.

WADE is impulsive. He makes decisions without giving them too much thought. He's thinking of being a flight attendant because he likes the way they dress.

ANDY usually leaves things to fate. He plans to hitch a ride to California after graduation, just to see what happens.

ELENA is compliant. She usually lets someone else make her decisions. Her parents think she should be a stenographer, so that's what she probably will do.

HAROLD procrastinates. He puts off decisions until the last minute. He plans to think about his future after graduation.

YOKO agonizes over every decision. She examines each alternative so closely — and so repeatedly — that she never seems able to make up her mind. She says she wants to interview several dozen more people before selecting a career path.

ARTURO makes decisions intuitively. Some things just feel right, he says. He's always liked the idea of being a wildlife biologist, but he isn't exactly sure what they do.

KENISHA has a rational approach to making decisions. She considers the alternatives, the pros and cons of each, and the likelihood of succeeding before making her choice. She is interested in technology and sees a bright future in computer-related careers, so she plans to train for a job in that field.

Which of these patterns do you use most often? Explain.

_____

_____

_____

Write your own definition of success here:

_____

_____

_____

_____
your name

Throughout this book we will be talking about success. As you read about and ponder this concept, make sure to keep **your own definition** in mind.

There Are Jobs . . . and There Are Careers

Although we often use the terms interchangeably, there is a difference between a *job* and a *career*. A job is a particular task or undertaking. It may be paid or unpaid. You will, undoubtedly, have many jobs during your lifetime.

But you will only have one career. Your career encompasses *all* of your life's work. You have already begun your career. The work you have done so far will help determine where you go from here. Future occupations grow out of past experiences. That is why people speak of career *development*. The path may not always be obvious, but the connections are there. So the choices you make now are important.

Making choices that are right for you is what this book is all about. Before you choose what you want, however, you need to know who you are. That is a subject we will tackle in the next chapter.

What lies behind us and what lies
before us are small matters compared
to what lies within us.
         —Ralph Waldo Emerson

Self-trust is the first secret of success.
                 —Ralph Waldo Emerson

CHAPTER TWO

Your Personal Profile

Getting what you want starts with knowing who you are.

Section One:
WHO AM I?

It was career night at Central High. When Letitia arrived, she found her friend, James, standing outside the gym, looking bewildered. "I didn't expect to find a scene like this," said James. The gym was packed with representatives from dozens of colleges and vocational schools. All branches of the armed forces were represented. And there were prospective employers and people working in a wide variety of careers.

"Isn't it great?" said Letitia. "Every one of those people stands for a possible future, a different way of life! But I guess it could be confusing. It's a good thing we have some ideas about what we want to do."

James cleared his throat and stared at his shoes.

"You do have some ideas, don't you, James?"

"Oh, sure," he replied. "My parents think it would be good for me to enlist in the army for a couple years. And Mr. Johnson, my chemistry teacher, thinks I should go into engineering. He wants me to talk to the admissions officer from his university. Of course, a lot of my friends are going to City College, and that might be fun."

"Yes, but what do you think? What kind of future do you want? You're the one who's going to be living there, you know. Have you considered who you are and what you want?"

"What's there to think about? I'm my parents' son and my friends' friend. I go to high school. I hang out. I'm just me. And who are you, if I may ask?"

"Well, I have thought about it," said Letitia. "In a lot of ways, I'm like you and my other friends. But people are like snowflakes or fingerprints — no two are the same. And it seems to me that it's the differences that make life interesting. We have to consider those things when we plan our lives.

"For example, I enjoy being on the debating team. I love to argue and discuss and try to persuade people, even though most of my friends think that kind of thing is boring. I'm also really interested in civil rights. So I'm thinking about being a lawyer, maybe even running for Congress someday. And those things, James, are all part of who I am."

Letitia has a head start on her friend, but it's not too late for James to consider who he is and what he wants to do. This is a process that can start at any time — and should continue throughout life.

Learning about yourself is a little like painting a picture. When you are very young, you have little more than a sketch — who takes care of you, what you like to eat, what you like to play with. As you grow and change, you learn more and more about yourself and begin to develop a vivid self-portrait. But the portrait is never complete. Some things will change. Many details will be added.

It's important, though, to keep a sort of running tab: "Who am I now? What's important to me at this point in my life? What do I do well? What do I most enjoy?" Your answers to these questions will help you make the decisions that will lead to a satisfying short-term future. By asking them again and again, you will be better able to make the necessary changes and adjustments that lead to a fulfilling life.

So, where do you start? The following exercise should help. Write your name in the center of the chart, then add as many words as you can that describe your own passions, values, strengths, and so forth.

As you fill out your chart, keep in mind that everyone has many different sides. Don't worry if some of your answers seem incompatible with others. Remember, too, that it's natural to want to "belong." Because you want to be like your peers, you may try to deny any interests or abilities that are not shared with your friends. But for this exercise — for your own sake — try to be complete and honest.

Don't get frustrated if you have a hard time completing your chart at this time. It will get easier as you work through this chapter. For now, do your best. Use a pencil so you can make any necessary changes as you go along.

Here are some short definitions to help you:

Passions: A passion is something you feel very strongly about, something for which you have boundless enthusiasm. You might be passionate about music, sports, art, computers, horses, cars, gardening, politics, the beach, marching bands, penguins — you name it. The happiest people are often those who find a way to incorporate their passions into their career. These are the people you'll hear say things like, "I can't believe they pay me to do this."

Values: Your values are those qualities or things that are most important in your life. Some people may value family or security, while others place more importance on adventure or power. You might value beauty, knowledge, social justice, or independence. Your career and life choices should be compatible with your values if they are to bring true satisfaction.

Personality traits and strengths: Are you tactful? Bold? Sociable? Quiet? Thoughtful? Energetic? Funny? Sympathetic? Inquisitive? Reserved? Dramatic? Intelligent? List as many traits as you can.

Skills and aptitudes: What skills have you learned? What comes easily for you? Do you have a special talent for anything in particular? Are you good at working with your hands? Solving problems? Working with people?

Roles: Your roles are the different parts you play in your life. Most of these are temporary, though some can go on for many years. Right now, you are probably a son or daughter, a student, a friend. You might also be an employee, a sister or brother, a girlfriend or boyfriend, and so on.

Occupations and vocations: Here we mean both work you do for pay (occupations) and recreational activities (vocations). For example, you might be a grocery clerk, babysitter, flute player, cook, ballet dancer, skateboarder, or basketball player.

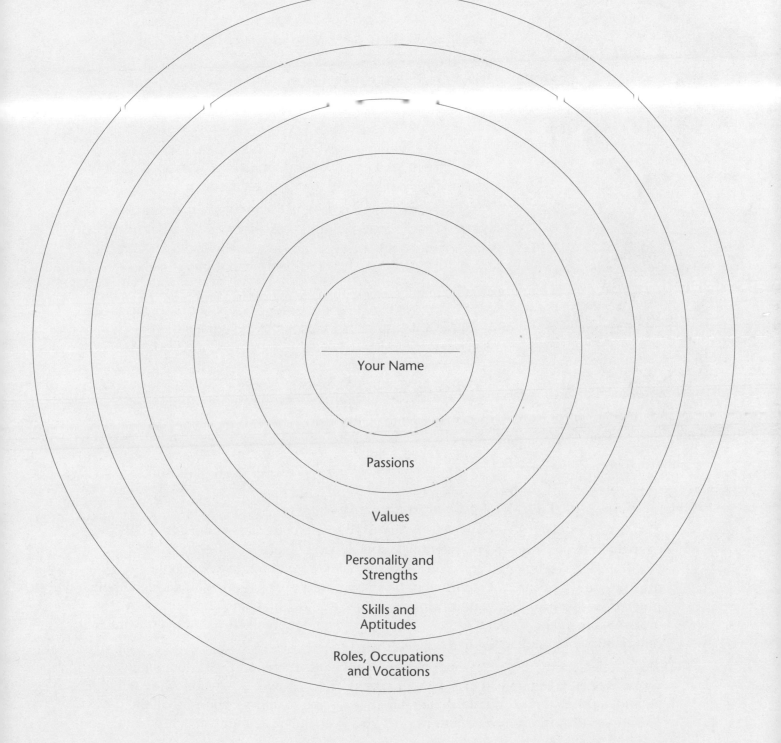

Your Name

Passions

Values

Personality and
Strengths

Skills and
Aptitudes

Roles, Occupations
and Vocations

Back at the gym, Letitia had just finished discussing law school admission requirements with a representative from the state university when James tapped her on the shoulder.

"Okay," he said, "you seem to know a lot more about this than I do. I don't know who to talk to or what questions to ask. Where do I start?"

"You can start by identifying your passions," she replied.

James grinned in what he imagined was a worldly and sophisticated way.

"That's not what I mean" said Letitia. "This is serious stuff. Aren't there things you really love to do? What could you do all day without getting bored or tired?"

"Well, last summer I taught my little brother and his friends how to play baseball and I really enjoyed that. I was in the school play and I guess I got kind of choked up when the audience gave us a standing ovation. I saw the movie Top Gun 14 times."

"That's a start," said Letitia. "What kinds of occupations does that list suggest? Do you want to be a teacher or a coach? Do you want to take acting lessons? Maybe you'd like being an Air Force or Navy pilot. Talk to some of the people here tonight about those possibilities. But you need to give your list more thought. Keep adding to it. See where it takes you. You want to be sure that, whatever you end up doing, you'll be able to fit in activities that give you that kind of natural high."

The dictionary defines passion as a "powerful emotion; boundless enthusiasm; deep, overwhelming feeling; or avid interest." Clinical psychologist Carl Goldberg says, "Passion is the energy and enthusiasm wedded to a sense of purpose that gives life meaning and pleasure." Preparing for a career is hard work. It takes time and patience. If you choose a field that you truly love, one that excites and energizes you, you will be motivated to *do* the work, to *find* the patience. You are more likely to stick with your plan and realize your goal.

The interests, activities, or accomplishments that cause this special feeling are different for everyone. It's up to you to discover your passions. Answering the following questions should get you started. But don't stop here. Be aware of your reactions to all the ordinary and extraordinary events in your life. Keep building your list.

Identifying Your Passions

These are some of the items on Letitia's list:

Winning a debate	Chocolate	Red shoes
Dancing	The Lakers	Long walks
Thunderstorms	Social justice	The Star Spangled Banner
Politics	Movies that make me cry	Writing

Complete the following statements. Don't be frustrated if you can't do it immediately.
But start being aware of these feelings. As more ideas occur to you in the next weeks,
turn back to this page and add them to your lists. You will continue to discover new
passions throughout your life.

My heart pounds with excitement when . . . .

_____

_____

I feel especially good about myself when . . . .

_____

_____

I get a lump in my throat when . . . .

_____

_____

I lose track of time whenever I am . . . .

_____

_____

If I could be any person in history, I would be . . . .

_____

_____

When I dream about my future, I see myself . . . .

_____

_____

If I could change one thing about the world, it would be . . . .

_____

_____

When Letitia came home, her phone was ringing. "Sorry to bother you, but I have another question."

"Yes, James, what is it?"

"I did what you suggested," he said. "I talked to the Navy recruiter about being a pilot, and I also had an interesting conversation with an actor. But I feel kind of uneasy."

"What do you mean?"

"Well, I'd like to wear a uniform and get a bunch of medals and ride in parades and stuff, but being a fighter pilot is, like . . . dangerous, you know? And it would be fun to get fan letters and have my picture in magazines and all that. But the guy I talked to said it can take years before you even get a small part — some people never make it. And all that time, you have to take classes and go to auditions — and you still have to find some way to make money, you know? So I'm confused. Part of me would really like to do these things. But another part thinks it wouldn't be that great.'

"James, I think you have a values conflict here," said Letitia.

"What do you mean by 'values'?"

"Values are the standards or guiding principles that are most important to you. It sounds to me like you are seeking recognition, but you also need security. The careers you're considering are risky. You may not feel comfortable in those roles. What you need to do now is figure out what your strongest values are, and then think about careers that are compatible. Be sure that the values are yours, though. Don't just try to please others. If you aren't really committed to your goal, you won't be able to take the necessary risks or feel good about what you are doing while you're in school or just starting out. This is something you really need to think through on your own, James."

VALUES SURVEY

What are *your* values? Is having plenty of time to spend with friends and family important to you? Or would you rather be off on some kind of adventure? Do you want to help other people? Do you want to exercise power? The following exercise should give some indication of what you value most. For each statement below, check the column that comes closest to matching your feelings.

		Very True	Some-Times True	Not Sure	Not True
1.	I'd rather donate to a good cause than join a prestigious club.				
2.	I'd rather have good friends than a lot of money.				
3.	I'd rather have my savings in a bank account than in the stock market.				
4.	I'm too adventurous to be tied down by a family.				
5.	I'd like a job where I set my own hours.				
6.	I enjoy books and movies in which the moral to the story is not obvious.				
7.	I'd rather be a scholar than a politician.				
8.	I would not want to work while my children are young.				
9.	I would rather write a fictional story than a research paper.				
10.	When I lend money to a friend, I don't worry about being paid back.				
11.	I'd rather be famous than wealthy.				
12.	I would rather associate with influential people than intellectual people.				
13.	Teachers should be paid as much as business executives.				
14.	I'd rather go to an art museum than a sporting event.				
15.	I will contribute to my retirement account before I buy extras.				
16.	I prefer jobs where the duties are varied and challenging.				
17.	I prefer jobs where the duties are consistent and goals are clear.				
18.	I feel a person's salary indicates how much he or she is valued on the job.				
19.	I would not want a high-powered job because it could strain my marriage.				
20.	It is important to me that my surroundings are attractive.				
21.	My reputation is worth more to me than all the money in the world.				
22.	I'd rather visit a place than read about it.				
23.	I'd rather *know* something than be *known for* something.				
24.	I'd rather have a secure job than a powerful one.				
25.	I'd like to be my own boss.				
26.	I believe a percentage of my income should be used to help others.				
27.	I would turn down a promotion if it meant I would have to travel away from my family too much.				

	Very True	Some-Times True	Not Sure	Not True
28. "Money talks."				
29. I would take a cut in salary if I were offered a position in the President's cabinet.				
30. I'd rather own a special work of art than a fancy car.				
31. I'd rather have time than money.				
32. I will always stop to watch a beautiful sunset.				
33. If my brother committed a crime, I would turn him in.				
34. I don't like to do things the same way all the time.				
35. My friendships are more precious to me than possessions.				
36. The fact that most careers that "help others" pay lower wages would not prevent me from entering these lines of work.				
37. It is important that I get recognition for what I do.				
38. I'd rather *work* for an exciting company than *run* a dull one.				
39. I would like to run for office in my community.				
40. I'd rather have my savings in a bank account than in the stock market.				
41. The first thing I would consider when deciding on a career is how much it pays.				
42. I always take time to be a good friend.				
43. The unpleasant aspects of feeding the hungry or caring for the sick would not bother me.				
44. I don't like to have my decisions questioned.				
45. I'd rather have a job with a high income than one with a lot of security.				
46. It is important for me to understand how things work.				
47. I like to organize activities for my friends and family.				
48. If I were famous, I would enjoy signing autographs.				
49. I'd rather have a secure job than an exciting one.				
50. Owning nice things is important to me.				
51. I like to do things my own way.				
52. I feel good when I volunteer my time to make my community a better place.				
53. I would never testify in court against someone in my family.				
54. It is important to me that my home is beautiful.				
55. I like to be in charge.				
56. I would rather work with other people than alone.				
57. Books and reading are important to me.				
58. I would stand up for my beliefs even if I were punished for it.				
59. I like to solve problems.				
60. I expect to be consulted when a group I am in is making a decision.				
61. If I believed strongly in a "cause," I would make it my first priority.				
62. I have expensive tastes.				
63. If a member of my family committed a crime, I would turn him or her in to the appropriate authorities.				
64. I don't like my friends to be too dependent on me.				
65. I'd rather be married than single.				

	Very True	Some-Times True	Not Sure	Not True
66. I like to make things.				
67. My appearance is important to me.				
68. I'd love to travel around the world alone.				
69. I am sensitive to colors that clash.				
70. Someday I'd like to own my own business.				
71. I'd rather be a leader than a follower.				
72. I'd rather follow someone else.				
73. I like to learn something new every day.				
74. I would never marry someone who had less money than I do.				
75. It is important that my mate is good looking.				
76. I would borrow money to go on a vacation.				
77. Charity begins at home.				
78. With enough money, I could be happy.				
79. I think it would be exciting to be famous.				
80. I value my privacy . . . I wouldn't want to be famous.				
81. I believe I should be home every night with my family and not out with friends.				
82. "Don't rock the boat."				
83. I would not take a job that I felt was unethical, no matter how much money it paid.				
84. I enjoy people who do things differently.				
85. I will go out of my way to help a stranger.				
86. I would like to have a building or street named after me.				
87. I would not lie even if telling the truth might hurt a friend's reputation.				
88. I'd rather live in a cabin in the wilderness than in a beautiful home.				
89. I like to look at problems from many different angles.				
90. It is important to me to be an influential person.				
91. I'd like to be known as being one of the best in my field.				
92. I like to try new things.				
93. I will not change my views just because they are unpopular.				
94. I think you should question "rules" if they don't make sense to you.				
95. I wouldn't want to travel alone.				
96. If asked, I would serve Thanksgiving dinner to the homeless and miss my family's celebration.				
97. I always stand up for what I believe in.				
98. I wouldn't like doing the same task all day long.				
99. I like to be called in an emergency.				
100. My family will be more important to me than my career.				
101. Trophies and awards are important to me.				
102. I like to help my friends with their problems.				
103. My title at work is very important to me.				
104. It is important to share my life with someone.				

33

Now assign a numerical value to each of your answers. Statements in the "very true" column are worth 9 points. Those you marked "sometimes true" get 6. Allow 3 points for each "not sure," and zero points for every "not true" answer.

In the columns below, write the numerical value of your response next to the statement number. For example, if you answered "very true" to the first statement, you would write a 9 on the line next to the number 1. When you have entered a number on each line, go back and total the columns under each heading.

ANSWERS

ADVENTURE	FAMILY	POWER	RECOGNITION
4. _____	8. _____	12. _____	11. _____
16. _____	19. _____	29. _____	37. _____
22. _____	27. _____	39. _____	48. _____
38. _____	53. _____	47. _____	79. _____
68. _____	65. _____	55. _____	86. _____
76. _____	77. _____	60. _____	91. _____
88. _____	81. _____	71. _____	101. _____
92. _____	100. _____	90. _____	103. _____
Total _____	Total _____	Total _____	Total _____

PERSONAL INTEGRITY and MORAL COURAGE	MONEY	SECURITY	CREATIVITY
21. _____	18. _____	3. _____	6. _____
33. _____	28. _____	15. _____	9. _____
44. _____	41. _____	17. _____	34. _____
58. _____	45. _____	24. _____	59. _____
63. _____	50. _____	40. _____	66. _____
83. _____	62. _____	49. _____	84. _____
93. _____	74. _____	72. _____	89. _____
97. _____	78. _____	82. _____	98. _____
Total _____	Total _____	Total _____	Total _____

HELPING OTHERS	KNOWLEDGE and TRUTH	FRIENDSHIP and COMPANION-SHIP
1. _____	7. _____	2. _____
26. _____	13. _____	10. _____
36. _____	23. _____	35. _____
43. _____	46. _____	42. _____
52. _____	57. _____	56. _____
85. _____	61. _____	95. _____
96. _____	73. _____	102. _____
99. _____	87. _____	104. _____
Total _____	Total _____	Total _____

BEAUTY and AESTHETICS	INDEPENDENCE and FREEDOM
14. _____	5. _____
20. _____	25. _____
30. _____	31. _____
32. _____	51. _____
54. _____	64. _____
67. _____	70. _____
69. _____	80. _____
75. _____	94. _____
Total _____	Total _____

In which category did you have the highest total? Right now, that value is most important to you. Remember, though, that values often change over time. You might want to come back to this survey every few years or when you are considering a change in your plans.

Did you have high scores in more than one category? If so, you might want to try to find a career that satisfies both or all your top values. If you value both beauty and adventure, for example, you might be happier tracking down international jewel thieves than you would be working in an art gallery or museum.

Each values category is described below:

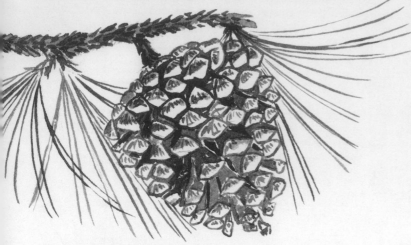

Power

Those who value power need to prepare for leadership. Usually, that means some type of advanced education or years of experience in your trade. Most political leaders, for example, have law degrees. Business leaders quite often have a master's degree in business administration. If you value power, make sure that any job you take offers room for advancement. Or consider starting a business of your own.

Adventure

If you value adventure, you would be happiest in a career that offers some degree of variety or unpredictability. You don't necessarily have to be a spy or a soldier of fortune, but you won't want a job with too much structure or routine. Since you are probably willing to take risks, you might make a good entrepreneur.

Family

Those who value family are usually happiest with careers that don't call for evening or weekend work or a great deal of travel. Flexibility is helpful, as is the opportunity to work at home. A career with a salary high enough to allow you to work part-time might be attractive.

Knowledge and truth

If you value knowledge and truth, you might find a career that lets you pass on your knowledge — teaching, for example, or being a librarian — rewarding. Or you might prefer a job that keeps teaching *you*: doing research, investigative reporting, and the like.

Personal integrity and moral courage

You will be most satisfied in a career that mirrors your sense of purpose if you value personal integrity and moral purpose. Perhaps your *field* of work is less important than what you do *within* that field. For example, if you are a lawyer, you would probably be more satisfied working in legal aid than in corporate law. It is important for you to feel that your work is worthwhile to society.

Money or wealth

Many career fields have the potential to pay very well. Make sure that the one you choose meshes with your other top values. If you also value security, for example, you might find it more satisfying to be an engineer than an entrepreneur. Remember, too, that you will probably need to spend the majority of your time working. Is there a job you would enjoy so much you wouldn't mind if it also had to be your hobby?

Friendship and companionship

If this is your highest value, you will want to make sure that your chosen career involves working closely with others. Things to consider: Would you prefer spending your time with co-workers or clients? Do you like to see the same faces every day, or would you like to meet new people on a regular basis? Do you have a circle of friends you want to reserve time for?

Recognition

You may be recognized by more people if you are a TV star than if you are the best caterer in town. But, generally, you can earn recognition in just about any field if you do your job well. Choose something for which you have the necessary skills or talents, and work hard.

Independence and freedom

If this is your highest value, you may find unstructured sales — real estate or insurance, for example — rewarding. In this type of job, you can set your own hours and work without constant supervision. You might prefer to work part-time, or you might want to be self-employed. Stay away from strict schedules or jobs in which you are constantly accountable to someone else.

Security

If you value security, you will be most comfortable in a job you know will be around for a while. No new companies or risky ventures for you. You may prefer to have clearly defined duties, rather than a loosely structured job.

Beauty or aesthetics

If this is your top value, *where* you work may be almost as important a consideration as *what you do*. Your setting must be one that you find visually attractive, whether it's a garden or a cathedral. You might want your work to center around beauty, as well — perhaps you'd be happy as a designer, an architect, or a florist.

Creativity

Creative people need room to exercise their imaginations, whether they are creating a work of art, inventing a better way to display merchandise, or solving a problem in computer programming. If this is your top value, you should seek a flexible career that lets you put your ideas to work.

Helping others

If you value helping others, there are many ways for you to accomplish your goal. The service industry, in fact, is one of the fastest growing parts of the economy. *How* do you want to help others? Some possibilities: you could be a paramedic, a physical therapist, a social worker, a nutritionist, a psychologist, a police officer, or a child care worker.

Strengths and Personality

James was waiting by Letitia's locker when she arrived at school the next morning. "Hi, James!" she said. "What a surprise. What's going on?"

"Well," said James, "I thought about my values, and I think I know what they are. I really would like to be recognized, to have people know who I am. I want to keep learning, to know about things. And I'd like some adventure in my life, too — as long as it's not too risky. I mean, I'd like to go to interesting places, but I'd rather not have people shooting at me on a regular basis, if you know what I mean. But what now? Values aren't jobs. I don't think anyone is going to hire me to be a well-known person."

"Probably not," Letitia agreed. "I guess the next step is to think about your passions and values and how they relate to your personality. How do you like to work? What are your strong points? How do you feel about this? How do you feel about that? Stuff like that."

"Okay," said James. "What do you think my strengths are?"

"Well, you're curious. You're not a bit shy. And you certainly are persistent! I'm late for class. Why don't you get some opinions from your other friends?"

Everyone has his or her own way of thinking, feeling, and acting. We are all unique. Our individual characteristics develop early in childhood and usually continue in a somewhat consistent manner throughout life.

In the four columns below, you will find a list of personality traits. Circle the 10 traits you feel best describe you.

a.	b.	c.	d.
forthright	enthusiastic	steady	analytical
adventurous	expressive	amiable	controlling
forceful	influencing	predictable	perfectionist
sharp	emotional	supportive	systematic
decisive	inventive	loyal	conventional
risk taker	spontaneous	methodical	respectful
demanding	trusting	team player	meticulous
authoritative	outgoing	calm	well-disciplined
direct	unselfish	thorough	diplomatic
curious	self-assured	dependable	precise
competitive	charming	self-composed	sensitive
self-sufficient	inspiring	possessive	accurate

Now total the number circled in each column:

_____   _____   _____   _____

People have a better chance of feeling successful when they know their own work style — including their strengths and their weaknesses. Understanding the way you are likely to behave on the job will greatly enhance your ability to choose a satisfying career and lifestyle.

The ancient Greek physician Hippocrates believed people exhibited four different behavioral styles. Today many career and profile tests also use four categories to distinguish types of behavior.

Complete the following self-evaluation quiz. Circle the letter under each situation that best reflects how you would be likely to act, feel, or think.

1. Your favorite projects are ones that are
   a. likely to have favorable results.
   b. enjoyable to take part in.
   c. clearly explained.
   d. detail oriented.

2. You are on the spring dance committee. You would be happiest
   a. chairing the committee.
   b. publicizing the event and selling tickets.
   c. decorating the hall.
   d. keeping track of the monies collected.

3. When doing your homework, you
   a. complete it in the shortest time possible.
   b. allow interruptions to take phone calls from friends.
   c. are willing to take time to help another student with the assignment.
   d. take time to check all your work for accuracy and thoroughness.

4. When faced with a stressful situation, you
   a. take charge and sometimes override the decisions of others.
   b. confront and may act in an impulsive fashion.
   c. become submissive and allow others to make your decisions.
   d. resist change and withdraw from the situation.

5. When getting dressed in the morning, you
   a. know exactly what you want to wear without giving it much thought.
   b. try on three things before deciding which is best.
   c. put on the clothes you laid out the night before.
   d. have no problem coordinating outfits because everything in your closet is in color sequence.

6. Your family is moving across the country to a lovely new home. You feel
   a. excited.
   b. curious.
   c. cautious.
   d. worried.

7. When you ask someone a question about a problem, you like an answer that
   a. is direct and to the point.
   b. includes stimulating ideas on various ways the problem could be solved.
   c. outlines the process for solving the problem.
   d. includes data and background on how the solution was reached.

8. When solving a problem, you are
   a. decisive.
   b. spontaneous.
   c. considered.
   d. deliberate.

9. When going shopping for clothes, you:
   a. will not need a list. If you forget something, you'll just get it later.
   b. buy whatever catches your eye. You don't worry how different outfits go together.
   c. have a list and visit every store in town before finalizing your purchases.
   d. know exactly what you want and have studied the newspaper for sales.

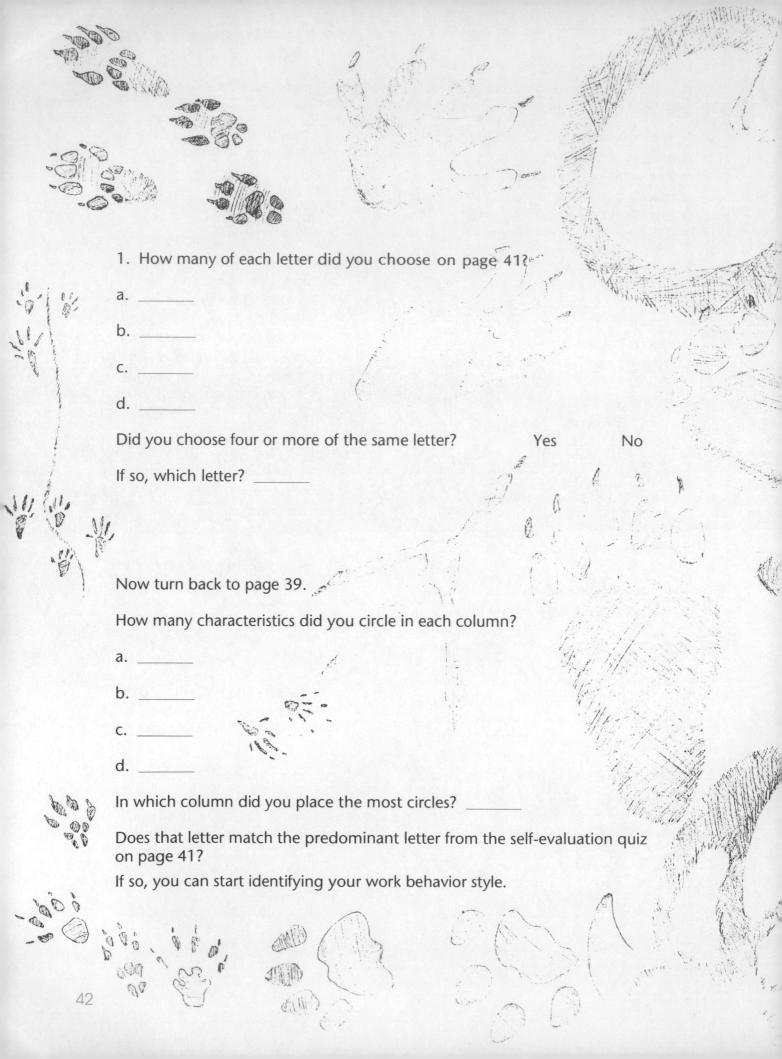

1. How many of each letter did you choose on page 41?

a. _____

b. _____

c. _____

d. _____

Did you choose four or more of the same letter?　　Yes　　No

If so, which letter? _____

Now turn back to page 39.

How many characteristics did you circle in each column?

a. _____

b. _____

c. _____

d. _____

In which column did you place the most circles? _____

Does that letter match the predominant letter from the self-evaluation quiz on page 41?

If so, you can start identifying your work behavior style.

The four styles are as follows:

a. Dominance

People with this behavioral style like to be in control of the work environment. They are decisive and focus on accomplishing goals. They work quickly and efficiently and like tasks that are challenging. They are usually happiest in leadership positions, such as manager, store owner, entrepreneur, school principal, contractor, office manager, and so on.

b. Influencing

These people's strength lies in their ability to influence others. They are good communicators and enjoy the relationships that they develop at work. Very personable, they want recognition and a stimulating work environment. They work best in a flexible setting. They are usually happiest in people-oriented jobs such as sales, marketing, teaching, counseling, coaching, customer service, and the like.

c. Steadiness

People in this category like tasks that have well-defined procedures. Known for their steadiness and follow-through, they excel at jobs calling for specialized skills. Maintaining relationships is a high priority for them, and their home life is important. Their decisions are considered, so they are often slower to accept change. They are usually happiest in specialized positions such as word processor, mechanic, assembly line worker, repairperson, lab technician, or scientist.

d. Compliance

This category of people is responsible for quality control. They are detail people who work from a prescribed set of rules and regulations. They enjoy systematic approaches to problems and strive for accuracy. They are very precise and are well prepared. They are happiest in "watch dog" jobs: working as accountants, law enforcement officials, editors, quality control managers, building inspectors, or zoning officials.

What you have worked through is a simplified approach to analyzing your work behavior style. Very few people exhibit only one of the four profile types. There are many different combinations. The intention of this exercise is to expose you to the concept and make you aware of the possibilities available to analyze your behavior patterns. As you become more serious about choosing your career path, you will probably want to take one of the more extensive, sophisticated tests available. Many corporations use these tests in helping employees evaluate how they best work and relate to others. If you have this knowledge now it should be helpful in your career planning search. We recommend the Personal Profile System from Carlson Learning Company.

Permission granted to adapt from the Personal Profile System by Carlson Learning Company®.

Your Strengths

Other things to consider in choosing an appropriate career are the strong points in your personality. Are you known to be friendly? Independent? Creative? Once again,, there are no "good" or "bad" traits. It's just a matter of choosing a career that's compatible and takes advantage of your strengths. For example, a friendly, outgoing person is likely to do better at and feel more satisfied with a job that provides an opportunity to make use of these social skills.

What are your strengths? It may be hard for you to list them. So get some help. One of the best ways to identify your strengths is to ask people who know you well. We all tend to be humble about such things, so your friends' and family's opinions may be more complete than your own. Ask at least six people what they feel your strengths are. It may be easiest to do this in a small group. At lunch today why not spend time discussing personality strengths with your friends?

Turn to page 39 for a list of terms that might apply. Some other strengths might be:

adaptable, ambitious, assertive, caring, charismatic, charitable, clever, cooperative, courageous, creative, dependable, empathetic, energetic, enterprising, friendly, gracious, gentle, handy, hardworking, humorous, independent, innovative, inventive, knowledgeable, nonconformist, nurturing, open-minded, persevering, protective, realistic, reliable, resourceful, sensitive, tactful, trustworthy, unusual, versatile, well-read, willing, etc.

Now complete the chart below. Choose eight of the personal strengths you have identified and list them in the first column. Then, in the second column, describe a situation or personal experience where you used these strengths or where they might be helpful.

I AM:	I HAVE USED THIS STRENGTH TO:
1.	
2.	
3.	
4.	
5.	
6.	
7.	
8.	
9.	
10.	

Skills and Aptitudes

Letitia was ready for James when she found him back at her locker that afternoon. She took a sign she'd made in art class from her purse and taped it to her locker door. "The Career Counselor Is In," it said, "Reasonable Advice at Reasonable Rates."

"Very funny," James said. "But you're the one who got me thinking about all this stuff. Who else am I going to ask?"

"Well, there is the counseling office. And the career center in the library. But I know those places can be kind of spooky sometimes. What can I do to help you?"

"I was just thinking. So far, we've talked about the kind of person I am, and the things I like to do. But aren't we overlooking something? Like what I'm able to do?"

"Oh, you mean your skills and aptitudes. Sure, they're important. At our age, of course, we've only begun to develop the skills we'll eventually need. But it's still a good idea to consider the things we can do now — especially the things we most enjoy."

"So where do I start?"

"Well, James, one way I've heard about is to list some of the accomplishments you're most proud of. You said you felt good about being in the play and teaching those kids how to play baseball. Take those experiences apart and think of the various skills you needed to succeed."

Though everyone has skills and aptitudes, many people are not good at recognizing them. Part of the reason for that is modesty — it seems boastful to announce that you are a terrific cook or a great musician. But there is also an element of truly *not thinking about* all the skills involved in planning a party or writing a paper. James's appearance in the school play, for example, required many different skills: he had to *read* the play, *convince* the director to give him the part, *interpret* that part, *memorize* his lines, *cooperate* with others in the play, *project* his voice, and *perform* in front of hundreds of people, to mention just a few.

Since you develop skills by performing them over and over again, they are likely to be things you enjoy doing. (If you didn't *like* twirling a dozen dinner plates on a stick balanced on the end of your nose, you probably wouldn't put in the hours necessary to become really good at it.) That makes recognizing them doubly important when you plan your career: skills are things you not only *can* do, but *enjoy* doing.

An aptitude, on the other hand, is something for which you have a natural talent or something that comes easily to you. If you can sketch an accurate portrait or landscape without much effort, you can be said to have an aptitude for art. If people say you are a "natural athlete," you probably have an aptitude for sports. You may not enjoy all the subjects or activities for which you have an aptitude, but you probably will. People tend to enjoy those things that they do well.

As Letitia reminded James, you will continue to acquire skills throughout your life. In addition, some people develop skills and recognize their aptitudes later than others. So don't be discouraged if your list seems short right now. The fact that you have never built a house doesn't mean that you should give up your dream of being a carpenter.

Name That Skill

Use the following exercise to begin the list of skills you've mastered. Write three accomplishments that gave you the most satisfaction, or that you're most proud of, on the lines below. Then, in the middle column, list the skills you used in that enterprise. If you have a hard time identifying these skills, describe the experience to friends or family members and ask them to help you. (You'll complete the last column later.)

Accomplishment	Skills Required	Skills Catagory D, P, or T
1.		
2.		
3.		

Do you see any pattern in the kinds of skills you used? (Did they involve physical strength or coordination? Numbers or equations? Reasoning? Dealing with people?)

Skills Identification

The *Dictionary of Occupational Titles (DOT)*, published by the U.S. Department of Labor, divides all job skills into three categories, based on whether they are used with data, people, or things. Data refers to information or instructions, and includes numbers, reports, statistics, and so on. People skills are used with co-workers, clients, or the public: persuading them, teaching them, and so on. Skills with things (machines, materials, finished products, and the like) include everything from packing them or putting them away to inventing or constructing them.

The DOT identifies the basic job skills as follows:

DATA	PEOPLE	THINGS
synthesizing	mentoring	setting up
coordinating	negotiating	precision working
analyzing	instructing	operating-controlling
compiling	supervising	driving-operating
computing	diverting	manipulating
copying	persuading	tending
comparing	speaking-signaling	feeding-offbearing
	serving	handling

Review your list of skills on the previous page. In the far right column place a D next to any skill used with data or information. Place a P next to those skills used with people and a T next to those used with material, equipment, or products. Do you seem to have a preference for any one skill category?

Use the chart below to list additional skills you currently have working with data, people, or things.

DATA	PEOPLE	THINGS

Can you think of skills you have not yet acquired that you would like to learn? List them below.

_____

_____

Roles, Occupations, and Vocations

The final ring on your chart asks you to list the roles, occupations, and vocations you now hold. These are very much a part of who you are. But they will change repeatedly as you get older. Today you may be someone's grandchild, for example. And some years down the road, you may be someone's *grandparent*. You will have other roles in between.

The difference between roles and occupations or vocations is simple. A role is what you *are* (son, daughter, sister, brother, friend, and so on). It requires no specific actions on your part. (It might be *nice* if you spent an hour playing nintendo with your little brother every night, but you will still be his brother or sister if you don't.) An occupation or vocation relates to what you *do*. It is something you spend time on. Occupations are paid employment. You may also be paid for your vocations, but not necessarily. A vocation is more like a special skill, something you are particularly suited to do. Right now, you are probably a student. You may have other vocations or an occupation as well (waiter or waitress, clerk, cashier, gas jockey, basketball player, musician, artist, and so on). These are more easily changed or taken away. If you don't show up for practice, you may not be a basketball player for long.

Record your present roles and occupations or vocations on the chart on page 27.

The Message Center

The next time Letitia saw James, he didn't seem his enthusiastic self. "Hey, James," she said, "are you okay? How's the career plan working out?"

"Oh, I don't know," he replied. "I thought about it a lot. And I finally hit on something I think I'd really like — broadcast journalism. But who do I think I'm kidding? I could never do that."

"I don't see why not," Letitia said. "You can talk. You can read. And the rest of it you'll learn in college."

"Come on, Letitia. Can you imagine me on TV? No one in my family has ever even gone to college. My mom's always told me to remember where I belong. And my dad says I'm nothing but a dreamer. I guess they're probably right. I'd never make it."

"You're right. With that attitude you never will find a way to create a future! Are you telling me your parents' fears and negative feelings are going to determine the way you feel about yourself?"

"You don't understand."

"Don't I? My father has always assumed that my brother would go to college. But not me. I'm the pretty one, he says. All I'm expected to do is get married. Sometimes I think he's right, that I'll never get into law school. But my mom believes in me. She says I can do anything I set my mind to, within reason. And I tell myself she's right. I think it's truly reasonable for you to believe you can go to college and make your dream come true.

"I know it's hard to give up those negative messages. But you've got to believe in yourself, James."

"Do you really think I could make it in TV news?" he asked.

"James, I think if you really commit yourself and give it all you've got, your chances are very high. You have the talent. If you're willing to work diligently, with no guarantee of success, I think you can make it."

We all get messages about who we are and what we should be doing from the important people in our lives. Family, teachers, friends — all let us know in various ways what they think. Some messages are hard to miss. If your father added your name to the sign on the family business the day you were born, there's not much doubt where *he* thinks your future lies. More subtly, a parent who always steps in to help you finish your homework, or rewashes the floor as soon as you put your mop away, gives the message that you are not competent to do something yourself.

Messages like these are limiting and destructive. They can make you feel that you have few choices in life, or that you just don't measure up. Other messages — like Letitia's to James, or her mother's to Letitia — are positive and empowering. They can build your confidence and help you achieve your dreams.

It's important to recognize the messages you get from your significant others because they are powerful and pervasive. They are like tapes playing over and over in the back of your mind, and they are difficult to erase.

Negative or limiting messages may come back to haunt you throughout your life, especially in certain situations. For example, if you've been given the message that you are too shy to have fun at parties, a little voice will crop up every time you get an invitation: "I'm no good at parties. I don't want to go." If you are aware of this fact, however, you can learn to dismiss the message and act more freely: "Thank you for sharing that. But I think I *will* go to the party and have a good time."

What messages have *you* received? For the following exercise, write what you think the significant people in your life would tell you about your future. Imagine them leaving their messages on your telephone answering machine.

Hello, you have reached _____'s message center. What would you like to tell me about my future? BEEP!

Mother's message: _____

_____

Father's message: _____

_____

Teacher's message: _____

_____

Other significant adult's message (coach, mentor, boss, relative): _____

_____

_____

Best friend's message: _____

_____

Girlfriend or boyfriend's message: _____

_____

Some of the strongest messages we receive come from society. Sex, age, race, nationality, religion, physical appearance, physical or intellectual abilities, financial status, social class — any of these can be the basis for taunts and jeers or praise and affection, great expectations or limited hope. What messages has society given you?

Society's message:

_____

_____

_____

Now go back and circle the messages that are limiting or negative. How much importance should you place on other people's opinions of you and their plans for your life? Should you have to live up to other people's goals and ideals? Who's life is it, anyway?

What positive messages can you give yourself about your future? Write them below. Recite them to yourself often. Or read them into a tape recorder and play them again and again while you're relaxing.

1. _____

_____

2. _____

_____

3. _____

_____

4. _____

_____

5. _____

_____

When you have completed all the exercises in this chapter, go back to page 27 and add what you've learned about yourself to the diagram there.

Who you are, of course, cannot be summed up by a bunch of words on a chart. You are a complex and constantly changing person, an individual unlike any other who's ever existed. The exercises in this chapter should, however, provide some insights that can help you make sound decisions for your future. The next step is deciding what you want.

There is only one success — to be able to
spend your life in your own way.
        —Christopher Morley

Happiness is not a state to arrive at, but
a manner of traveling.
        —Margaret Lee Runbeck

CHAPTER THREE

Lifestyles of the Satisfied and Happy

Keeping your balance and perspective

Section Two:
WHAT DO I WANT?

Deciding what you want from life is not an easy task. What you want today is probably quite different from what you wanted 10 years ago. And, in another 10 years, your wants may well have changed again. That's to be expected. What you want usually depends on who you think you are at the time. As you change, so do your needs and desires.

In general, though, most people want happiness, peace, and life satisfaction. But the things that will *give* them these feelings vary greatly. Contrary to popular opinion, money and outward signs of success don't have much to do with life satisfaction. That comes from *inside*, from your own unique achievements and sense of self.

Again, though, these will change. Perhaps this section of the book should be titled "What Do I Want *Now*." This is something you need to reevaluate on a regular basis. The processes you'll learn in the following chapters should help.

To paraphrase Mick Jagger, "You can't get what you want 'til you get what you need." Fortunately for us, someone has already determined the things we all need in order to be fully satisfied — and the order in which we must have them. The psychologist Abraham Maslow developed what has come to be called the Maslow Triangle. It graphically illustrates this hierarchy of human needs.

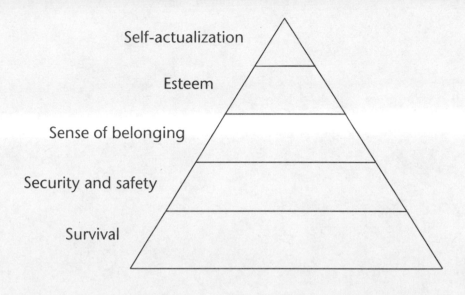

It's important to become familiar with this diagram. Deciding what you want from life is difficult. If you can place yourself on a particular level of the triangle, you will have a better understanding of what you need to do next.

Think of the triangle as a ladder, with the bottom rung at the triangle's base. You cannot jump over a rung or two. You must take each step in order if you want to reach the top. (It's quite possible to slip down the rungs, however.) But let's not get ahead of ourselves. Let's look at the triangle.

According to Dr. Maslow, our first need is simply to **survive**. We must have food and water, clothing, and shelter. Until we have these basic necessities, we cannot move on to consider our next need, which is for **safety and security**. The first two rungs deal only with physical and emotional survival — not a very satisfying way to live for most people.

When you hit the third level of the triangle, your need for other people becomes apparent. Some people are more dependent on relationships than others. But we all need to feel connected to other human beings. We all need to have a **sense of belonging**.

As we near the top of the triangle, we find that we have a need for **esteem**. We want other people to feel that we are worthy of respect. We also want to respect ourselves. At this point, we become capable of thinking about what we want, rather than simply about what we need.

Finally, at the peak of the triangle, is the need for what Maslow calls **"self-actuali-zation."** Self-actualized people are those who have done what they set out to accomplish, who have reached their goals. Not many people reach this point. (Only about 10 percent.) And not everyone who gets there stays there. Some people continue to set new goals every time they reach their old ones.

Other people can quickly slide back to a lower rung. For example, people who lose their jobs or their health may find themselves back seeking survival and safety. Until they reachieve these needs, they cannot approach — or probably even give much thought to — their higher needs.

As you think about your current place in the hierarchy of needs, it is important to remember that achieving life satisfaction is a *process*. It can only be accomplished one step at a time.

So be patient with yourself. It may be years before you can say exactly what you want from life. Even then, you may change your mind. The world is full of middle-aged people who are still trying to decide what they want to be when they grow up.

But the process of thinking about your identity and your future can be rewarding in itself. It can get you headed in the right direction. It can help you realize that you have some control over your life.

Where Are You Now?

Answer the following questions to determine your present location on the Maslow Triangle. If you answer yes to the questions in each section, color in the corresponding section on the triangle below.

SURVIVAL

Do you have enough food and water to survive?	Yes	No
Do you have a place to live?	Yes	No
Do you have enough clothes to keep you warm?	Yes	No

SECURITY AND SAFETY

Do you feel safe?	Yes	No
Do you feel secure?	Yes	No

SENSE OF BELONGING

Do you feel you belong somewhere?	Yes	No
Do you feel loved?	Yes	No

SELF-ESTEEM

Do you feel good about yourself?	Yes	No
Do you feel worthwhile or valuable as a human being?	Yes	No

SELF-ACTUALIZATION

Do you feel accomplished?	Yes	No
Do you feel mature?	Yes	No
Do you trust your judgment?	Yes	No
Do you feel in control of your life?	Yes	No

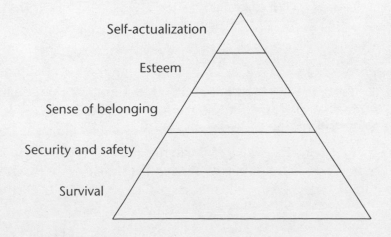

How Do You Want to be Remembered?

Walter Johnson always seemed to be three steps ahead of everyone else. When other children his age were learning to crawl, Walter was learning to roller skate. "A much more efficient means of transportation," he explained to his mother.

At five, Walter was memorizing Homer's Odyssey — in Greek. "Such a musical language," he said. Few people were surprised when Walter graduated at the top of his college class at age 14.

But even his mother was shocked to find 16-year-old Walter carving his own tombstone in the family basement. "What are you doing!" she exclaimed. "Are you sick? What's going on? You have to tell me!"

"I'm fine, Mom," he said. "No sense putting this off until the last minute. Besides, I have a use for it now. I need it to show me how to live."

"What do you mean?" she asked.

"I've carved it right here — what I want to be remembered for. For now, it will be my guide. It will help me make decisions and make the best use of my time."

He held up the stone. WALTER JOHNSON, it said. HE GAVE IT HIS BEST SHOT.

It may seem odd, but Walter's idea is a good one. One of the best ways to determine what you really want out of life is to think about how you want to be remembered after death. Caught up in the demands of day-to-day living, we often lose track of our fondest dreams, our mission in life, our legacy.

We all want to be recognized or acknowledged for some action, way of being, or accomplishment. This is a basic human need. Taking the time now to think about the contribution you would like to make in your lifetime will help give your life direction.

60

How would you like to be remembered? Do any of these epitaphs strike a chord?

JACK LITTLE: BEST COOK IN CHICAGO

LINDY WELTER: EVERYBODY LOVED HER

GEORGE JAKES: A NEW CAR EVERY YEAR

BERTA SANTINI: CRUSADER FOR JUSTICE

EDWARD PEARCE: HE MADE PEOPLE LAUGH

MARY JO THOMPSON: FIRST WOMAN PRESIDENT OF THE UNITED STATES

WILBUR SANFORD: TEACHER OF THE YEAR

LUCY BARTON: PROUD OWNER OF 139 PAIRS OF SHOES

CONNIE FITZPATRICK: WORLD TRAVELER

LEWIS JONES: PEACEMAKER

ROBERTA ZIMMER: SUPERSTAR

HAROLD CLAUSSEN: FAMILY MAN

MARGARET GONZALES: PHILANTHROPIST

LEE CHUNG: POET

In the space below, write your own epitaph. How do you want to be remembered? At the end of your life, what would you have to have done in order to be thought of that way? You don't have to limit your answer to a single line, but keep it brief.

Try not to get hung up on external forms of success, such as making a million dollars. You are more likely to be remembered — and to feel good about yourself — because of what you do with the money. If you must have that million, consider how you would use it. Would you set up a scholarship fund? Build a wing of a hospital? Assure the future security of your family? Save the whales? Retire and become a community volunteer?

Consider your personal heroes. These might be world figures like Nelson Mandela or Mohandas Gandhi, or they might be known only to a few such as the coach who made you believe in yourself or the stutterer who landed the lead in the class play. What do these people tell you about your values?

Think about your passions and your dreams as well. And remember that, unlike Walter's, *your* mission is not carved in stone. It may change as you continue to grow.

_____ : _____

      Your name

                           _____

                           _____

Your Lifestyle

As you may be beginning to see, your career choice will affect more than the 40 hours a week you'll spend on the job. A job title often suggests a whole way of life. Rock star, scientist, farmer, carpenter — when we think of people in these occupations, we immediately visualize what they wear, where they live, who their friends are, perhaps even the person they voted for in the last election. (We may be *wrong*, mind you. But, in general, you won't find too many farmers in Manhattan. And most scientists are not close personal friends of Michael Jackson.) In short, your career will help define your lifestyle.

What do we mean when we talk about lifestyle? Until recently the word didn't even appear in the dictionary. But sociologists and psychologists have come to realize that the way people live, the way they think and feel, what's important to them, and how they spend their time, money, and energy help explain not only individual lives, but how and why our society works the way it does. The term *lifestyle* is a composite of your income and education, your attitudes, your political and spiritual beliefs, where you choose to live, how you earn and spend your money, what is most important to you — even how secure and happy you are likely to be.

Before you begin researching possible careers, it is important to try to determine what type of lifestyle you want. Your career choice will have a great impact on the type of lifestyle you will lead.

COMPONENTS OF LIFESTYLE

Lifestyle has many components. We've listed some below. Think about your ideal future life and complete this questionnaire as best you can.

RELATIONSHIPS

Do you want to be married? _____ Have children? _____ If so, how many? _____

What kinds of people would you like to be your friends? _____

_____

How much time (hours per week) will you want to spend with your family? Your friends?

_____

WORK

How much time do you want to spend at your chosen profession? Less than 20 hours per week? 20 – 40 hours per week? 40 – 50 hours? As long as it takes?

_____

What is your mission in life? What sort of commitment do you want or need to make to some larger goal?

_____

PERSONAL

How much time each week would you like to spend on:

Recreation _____ Individual pursuits _____

Contemplation and relaxation _____

How much flexibility do you want in your life? _____

What will be the "pace" of your life? Are you a high-energy person who always needs to have many projects at once or are you a person who likes to tackle one thing at a time?

_____

How will you meet your spiritual needs? _____

MATERIAL ITEMS

Where do you want to live? Describe the location and housing. _____

_____

What income level would you like to reach? _____

Describe the possessions you want most. _____

Happiness is a Balanced Lifestyle

Emma is a stockbroker who is totally dedicated to her work. She seldom gets home before 10 at night, and is back at her desk by 7:00 A.M. She devotes her weekends to reading annual reports and books and articles dealing with her job. She hasn't taken a vacation in five years and has no close friends or outside interests.

Isaac is a police officer in a small town. He and his wife have two children. He volunteers at a homeless shelter two nights a week and coaches his daughters' softball team. In order to save money, Isaac and his wife are renovating their house by themselves. He attends night school, working toward a degree in criminology. Issac is also a guitarist with a small band that plays for local social events. He tries to do his share of the housework and thinks it's important to spend time with his children each day. Isaac and his wife go out alone at least once a week. His parents are getting older, and he likes to see them often. He enjoys going out with his friends.

Emma and Isaac have little in common — except that both have problems balancing their lives. Emma's life is incomplete. There are times when it is necessary to center your attention on one part of your life (finishing a project at work or recuperating from an illness, for example). But Emma may never be truly happy if she keeps up her current pattern indefinitely. She needs to look at Maslow's Triangle.

Isaac is probably already aware that *his* life is *too* full. Some people have enormous amounts of energy and are able to juggle a wide variety of interests, activities, and responsibilities. But there are only 24 hours in a day. And everyone has to sleep *sometime*. Isaac needs to decide which activities are most important to him and which ones he can most easily give up.

The exact makeup of a balanced lifestyle will be different for everyone. Some people want to give most of their attention to their work. For others, family is most important. Some people want or need to give priority to health concerns. But, in general, an emotionally and physically healthy life will include time for the following:

Physical health: Time to sleep and eat wisely must be built into every balanced lifestyle. Healthy people need time for both exercise and relaxation. Other health needs vary.

Work: Work is a central activity and source of identity for most adults. How important is it for you? Will you work part-time? Full-time? More than 40 hours a week? Would you like to be able to take time out when you have small children?

Family/relationships: Will you marry and have children? Marry and *not* have children? Surround yourself with a group of close friends? Today, there is a wide range of acceptable ways to meet your needs for close relationships with others. Your best choice might depend on the weight you give other parts of your life. For example, Emma (above) would almost certainly be happier if she had good friends and a circle of acquaintances she could socialize with regularly. Whether she would be happy marrying a man with three children is questionable.

Do you want to have children? They take time and attention, especially when they are young. How would you adjust your lifestyle to accommodate them? For example, could you earn enough money working part-time? Could you work at home?

Leisure and recreation: Your balanced lifestyle should include time for hobbies, avocations, and the leisure activities that add so much to life. Will you travel? Have a garden? Follow your favorite sport or athletic team? Read or go to the movies?

Spiritual life: The dictionary defines spirit as "that which constitutes one's unseen, intangible being" or "the essential and activating principle of a person." Many people realize their spiritual needs through their religion. Others choose to "give something back" to the world by working as a volunteer or getting involved with organizations that promote conservation, peace, or human rights. Some people meet their spiritual needs privately, through meditation, reading, walking, and the like.

With all these considerations, it's easy to see how a life can get off balance!

The Modified Maslow Triangle

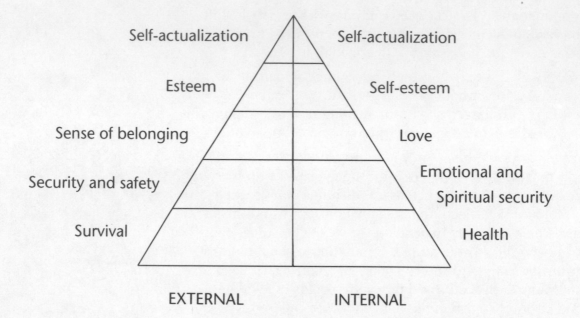

EXTERNAL	INTERNAL
Self-actualization	Self-actualization
Esteem	Self-esteem
Sense of belonging	Love
Security and safety	Emotional and Spiritual security
Survival	Health

To make it easier to visualize a balanced lifestyle, we have divided Maslow's Triangle down the middle. Although the hierarchy of needs remains the same, *our* triangle differentiates professional, or external, needs (shown on the left side) from personal, or internal, needs (diagrammed on the right).

> **Our external lives** include such things as careers, the tasks we do, the possessions we accumulate, the roles we play, and the way others see us. Our social and educational systems teach us to deal almost exclusively with this side of life.

> **By internal lives,** we mean our physical and spiritual well-being, our values, and our personal relationships. This is the side of life society tends to ignore. This may account for the increased use of drugs, depression, divorce, and general discontent we are experiencing today.

If either side is given too much emphasis, our lives become unbalanced. Life satisfaction decreases. It is possible on our double triangle to achieve one level of fulfillment in career life and quite another in personal matters. The happiest people are those who engage in both aspects of life. They are less willing to sacrifice one part for the sake of the other.

But it's often a difficult balancing act. Today, especially, men and women attempting to mix career and family are having problems finding the time for all the important activities in their lives. To plan wisely, if you see both career and family in your future, you might want to read *MORE CHOICES: A Strategic Planning Guide for Mixing Career and Family* (Bingham and Stryker, Advocacy Press).

Let's go through our divided triangle, level by level. It's necessary to repeat ourselves somewhat, so please be patient.

Just as the most basic external need is for **food and shelter** (left), **good health** is the most basic personal need (right). Until we have these, we are unable to satisfy the next level of needs — **financial and physical safety** on the left side, **spiritual** and **emotional security** on the right side. It is impossible for most people to experience life satisfaction unless they reach these first two levels of fulfillment. Yet many people begin to make trade-offs here. They sacrifice their health in order to make more money even though, without good health, they cannot hope to enjoy their lives.

Those who feel confident of the ability to support themselves — without giving up physical or emotional health — can move on to the next level of need: **love** (on the right or personal side) and **belonging** (on the left or professional side). Although it is important to "belong," to have a circle of acquaintances and casual friends, it is also necessary to have at least one deeper relationship. This might be with a spouse, a best friend, or someone else to whom you feel particularly close and committed.

People who do not have satisfying relationships with others cannot move on to achieve **self-confidence** and **achievement** (on the external side) and **self-esteem** (an internal need). At this level, you like yourself and feel good about what you are doing. Again, we see the necessity to consider the needs on both sides of the triangle. You might feel confident of your ability to succeed by cheating, lying, or manipulating, but if success comes at the expense of your self-esteem, it is not likely to make you happy. Shortcuts, even when successful, carry costs that will lessen good feelings.

Once you have attained both confidence and self-esteem, you are on your way to becoming one of those rare **self-actualizers**, someone who is satisfied and happy with her or his life.

How can you tell if you are neglecting one side of your life? Besides the obvious ways — losing your health, your job, your close relationship — listen to your inner voice. Be aware of your feelings. Do you ever begin sentences with phrases such as "if only," "I wish," "I should but I can't," or "If I had the time I would"? These are clues that your life is not as satisfying as it might be. It's time to take a closer look and make some changes.

Let's see what Emma's and Isaac's diagrams might look like:

Emma has a good job and the respect of her colleagues and superiors. She thinks her work is of value, and loves what she does. Because she puts in so many hours, however, she has no time for personal relationships or private interests, and the stress of her job has placed her health in jeopardy. Emma's triangle looks like this:

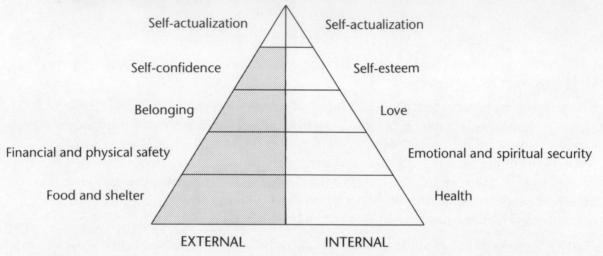

Isaac, too, has a good job and the respect of his community. He feels good about working toward his degree in criminology. He loves his wife and children and has many friends. But he seems to be exhausted all the time because of all he does. And he gets down on himself because he can't always do what he's promised. Many of his projects are done haphazardly or not completed. Isaac's triangle looks like this:

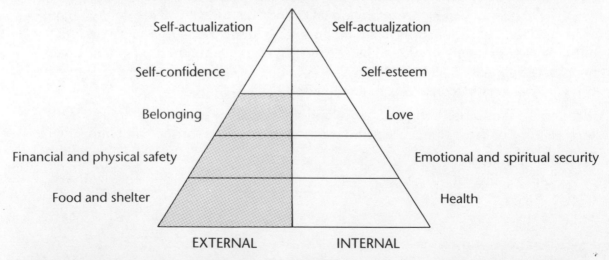

Especially when you don't make conscious changes in your life, things can get off kilter over time. That's why it is important to reevaluate your situation regularly and try to become more aware of your feelings.

When Joanie was 25, she had a financially secure job that she loved, the respect of her fellow workers, and a circle of devoted and loving friends. Shade the triangle below to represent the levels had Joanie attained in both her professional and personal life.

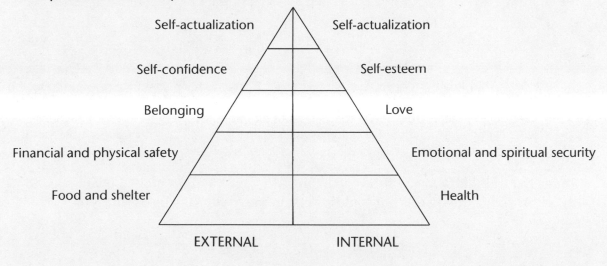

By the time she was 30, things had changed. Her job seemed less satisfying, though she put in many hours. The resulting stress caused health problems. Many of her friends had married and started families or moved away to take new jobs, and Joanie's social life was much reduced. She thought she might like to have a family of her own, but she wasn't dating anyone at the moment. Shade this triangle to show how Joanie's life had changed.

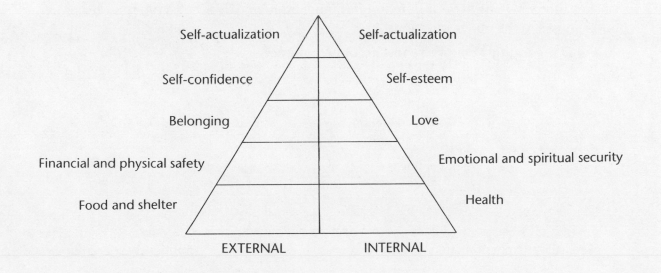

What About Your Life?

Describe your life right now:

How is your health? Do you get enough to eat? Do you have adequate housing? Do you feel financially secure and physically safe? Do you feel emotionally secure? Are your spiritual needs being met? Do you feel you belong to a group? Do you feel loved? Do you like yourself? Do you feel confident about your abilities and who you are? Are you satisfied and happy?

Shade the triangle below to show the balance in your life right now. Do you need to make any adjustments? What could you do to make your life more satisfying?

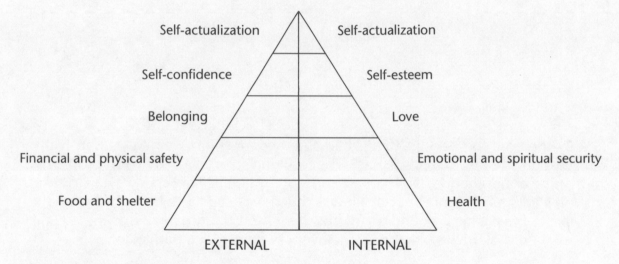

Now interview one of your parents or another adult you know and interpret his or her responses to the above questions.

Shade the triangle below to show his or her balance.

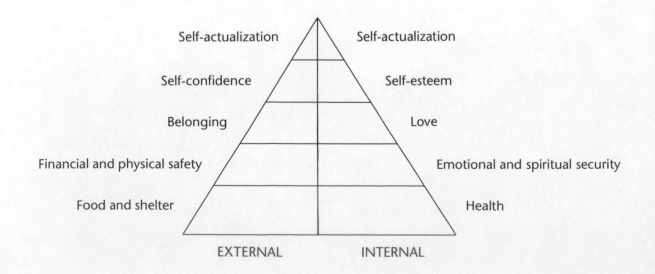

What do you think the triangle of a homeless person living alone would look like?

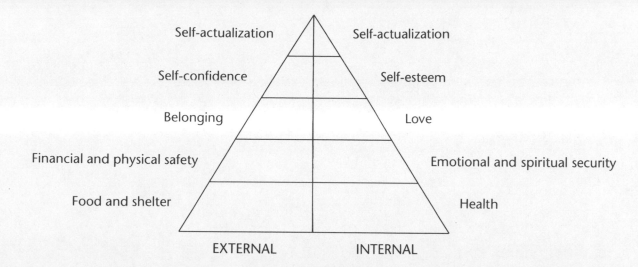

Self-actualization   Self-actualization

Self-confidence   Self-esteem

Belonging   Love

Financial and physical safety   Emotional and spiritual security

Food and shelter   Health

EXTERNAL   INTERNAL

Your desired lifestyle is something to be considered when making career decisions. As you will see in the next chapter, however, any way of life you choose involves costs as well as rewards. These might relate to finances, psychological rewards or sacrifices, or the degree of commitment required.

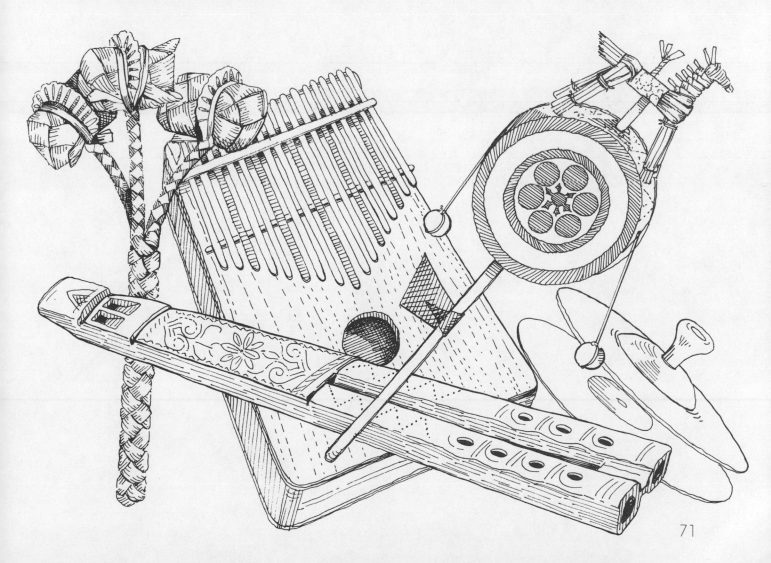

It's good to have money and the things money can buy, but it's good too, to check once in a while and make sure that you haven't lost the things that money can't buy.
                                        —George Horace Lorimer

I'd rather have roses on my table than diamonds on my neck.
                                        —Emma Goldman

CHAPTER FOUR

What Cost This Lifestyle?

Every career choice involves sacrifices
and rewards.

Ralph Tuttle, young business reporter for the <u>Daily Bugle</u>, was upset. His interview with Ivy Elms, the highest paid executive in the world, was not proceeding as expected. This was supposed to be Ralph's big chance. He could almost see the headline: IVY ELMS REVEALS SECRETS FOR SUCCESS TO JUNIOR REPORTER. Instead, the famous executive was running on about things that made no sense to Ralph. Was she senile? Ralph cheered up a bit. Maybe that was another angle he could use for his story.

"Making a lot of money can be one of the most expensive things in the world," Ivy said when Ralph tuned back in to the interview. "I'm lucky I can afford this job."

"Wow," Ralph thought. "The old girl really is going off the deep end." He decided to play along with her. "Just what do you mean by that, Miss Elms?"

Ivy poured herself a glass of mineral water from the crystal decanter on her enormous rosewood desk. She removed two tablets from a sterling silver pill box, explaining, "This one's for my blood pressure, and this is for my ulcer. Been taking them for years. Fortunately, I've never had any real health problems. Health is one of the first things a high-pressure job like this can cost."

Ralph's face brightened. "OH! I get it. You mean making a lot of money is expensive because of the other things you have to give up, right?"

"I knew you'd catch on sooner or later," Ivy said.

"So what else has your success cost you?"

"One of the sad things is that you never know exactly what your life might have been. No one ever knows that. So you just have to go after what seems most important. I always wanted to be a big success in business. This company has been my family, my best friend, my only hobby. I invested my life in it, you might say. I never married or had children — didn't think I could spare the time. Now I often wonder if people are nice to me only because they want something they think I can give them.

"This power to affect so many lives is a big responsibility. I worry about it. What happens if I make a mistake and profits fall and I have to lay some people off? There's no one else to blame. I also worry about leaving the company in good shape. All those young, ambitious people are waiting out there to take my job away from me. That makes me more determined, and then I work a little harder, which takes its toll on my health and my sense of humor.

"But I got what I wanted and, more or less, I'm happy with that. I live very well —beautiful homes, expensive cars, even a corporate jet. I'm known and respected all over the world. I have the pleasure of knowing that I do an important job, and that I do it better than anyone.

"But always remember, Mr. Tuttle, every job has its costs as well as its rewards. I have wealth, position, and power, but I will always wonder what it's like to have a family."

After the interview, Ralph asked himself what Ivy's story might mean for him. He thought about the way he lived and the way he'd like to live. How important was money to him, he wondered. What did he need to make his life meaningful? Ivy had set her goal early, and she stuck to her plan. She invested heavily in her career. Ralph thought about the commitment that called for and wondered if he was willing to follow through in the same way.

Nothing is ever enough when what you are looking for isn't what you really want.
—Arianna Stassinopoulos Huffington

75

Every job involves three different kinds of rewards — and sacrifices. The most obvious consideration is financial — how much money can you expect to earn at this job? Your salary will visibly affect your lifestyle. That is why it is essential to consider the cost — in dollars — of the material things you want to include in your life when making career decisions. Is it reasonable to expect that an elementary school teacher will be delivered to his classroom in a chauffeur-driven limousine?

The second consideration involves the physical, emotional, or psychological rewards and sacrifices of a given career. This concern is tied directly to your own values. What is most important to you? The idea is not to find a job that offers only rewards — as far as we can determine, no such job exists. But one person's reward may be a sacrifice to someone else. Being a politician, for example, may offer large rewards to someone who values recognition. For someone who values privacy, however, this career would require a big sacrifice. When you look at potential careers, consider both the rewards and the sacrifices and try to find one that matches your own values closely.

The third consideration is commitment. Do you want this job or lifestyle badly enough to invest the required time, money, and energy to prepare for it? Some people decide to scale down their dreams when they find they don't have the "stick-to-itiveness" to make them come true, or because they think the sacrifices are too great. For example, one man we know who grew up believing he would be head of a major corporation abandoned that plan to work for a smaller firm. The change allows him to pursue other interests and to have more time for family and community affairs. He thinks the trade-off was worthwhile.

This chapter is designed to help you determine just how much your dream lifestyle will cost: in money, in physical and emotional health, and in commitment.

To begin, you need to consider the income you would need to support your ideal lifestyle.

Your Budget

Let's talk about the kind of lifestyle you want to have — and how much money it is likely to cost. The following exercise asks you to make choices about everything from where you'd like to live to the vacations you'd like to take. Charts are provided to show approximately how much each choice costs (in today's dollars). Make your choice in each category, find the appropriate figure on the charts, and enter your monthly expense for each choice in the space provided.

Since the point of the exercise is to help you make career decisions for your future, don't base your choices on what you think is realistic for you right now. Instead, think of the way you would like to be living at some specific age in the future (make it at least 29 years old).

Choose an age and then complete this statement: Today I am _____ years old. In _____ years, when I am _____ years old, this is how I would like my life to look.

FAMILY PROFILE

The first choice you need to make concerns your future family. In the real world, this choice is not totally under your control. But dream away. Check the marital status you see for yourself at the age you've chosen, and the number of children you'll have, if any. Fill in the ages of your children.

MARITAL STATUS	CHILDREN	AGES OF CHILDREN
☐ Single	0 _____	_____
☐ Married	1 _____	_____
☐ Divorced	2 _____	_____
☐ Separated	3 _____	_____
☐ Widowed	4 _____	_____
☐ Other	5 _____	_____
	6 _____	_____

OTHER DEPENDENTS   WHERE I WOULD LIKE TO LIVE

_____   _____

_____   _____

_____   WHY?

_____   _____

Housing

Housing is the most expensive item on most people's budget. It is possible that your future spouse, a titled aristocrat, will inherit the family estate (tax-free, of course). But don't count on it. For the purpose of this exercise, assume that you will have to allot a portion of your income for a place to live.

Keep your own values in mind as you complete this exercise. It's *your* dreams we're interested in, not your mom's or your best friend's.

Do you want to live in:

☐ Government housing   ☐ A farm or ranch

☐ A rental apartment   ☐ A cabin

☐ A cooperative apartment   ☐ A luxury home/estate

☐ A rental house   ☐ No permanent home

☐ Your own home   ☐ Other _____

☐ A condominium

How many bedrooms? _____ Bathrooms? _____

Other distinguishing features _____

_____

Check the classified advertisement section of a newspaper to get an idea of the sales price of homes and rental rates. The charts on the next page may help you figure your monthly costs.

Monthly payment/rent	$ _____
Monthly property taxes	$ _____
Monthly insurance	$ _____
Total utilities/phone	$ _____
Housing	$ _____ [1]

Enter at [1] on page 92. Your Budget Profile

HOME AFFORDABILITY, CITY BY CITY

City	Median Household Income	Median House Price	House Affordability Ratio
Albany/Schenectady	$27,523	$89,300	31%
Birmingham	23,523	76,500	31
Boston	32,012	182,900	18
Chicago	30,190	99,300	30
Cleveland	27,933	69,900	40
Dallas/Fort Worth	30,902	85,500	36
Denver	32,724	83,500	39
Hartford	34,034	169,000	20
Honolulu	31,313	198,700	16
Indianapolis	27,852	66,700	42
Los Angeles	27,579	175,600	16
Louisville	26,036	54,600	48
Minneapolis/St Paul	32,444	84,300	38
New Orleans	24,489	73,200	33
Oklahoma City	26,061	56,900	46
Phoenix	28,057	79,100	35
St. Louis	29,330	79,500	37
Salt Lake City	27,742	66,400	42
San Francisco	32,538	196,300	17
Seattle/Tacoma	28,583	93,600	31
Washington, D.C.	39,865	131,600	30

Hint: The higher the affordability ratio figure, the easier it is to purchase a home. The annual income in Louisville purchases 48% of a typical home while the annual income in Los Angeles purchases only 16% of a median priced home. Source: National Association of Realtors

RENTING VERSUS OWNING

Location	Home Price	Monthly Costs Owning/Rental	
Los Angeles	$255,900	$2,508	$1,114
Philadelphia	183,600	1,880	860
Chicago	166,200	1,844	953
Atlanta	127,600	1,398	777
Houston	77,600	$995	599

Note: figures based on median three-bedroom house with 2 1/2 baths and 1,900 square feet.

Source: *U.S. News & World Report,* April 17, 1989.

MONTHLY MORTGAGE PAYMENTS IF INTEREST IS:
(assuming 20% down payment)

Price	8%	10%	12%	Insurance	Taxes
$40,000	$235	$281	$329	$8	$27
60,000	352	421	494	12	40
80,000	470	562	659	16	53
100,000	587	702	823	20	67
120,000	705	843	988	24	80
140,000	822	983	1,152	28	93
175,000	1,028	1,229	1,441	34	117
200,000	1,174	1,405	1,646	40	133
300,000	1,762	2,107	2,470	60	200

FIRST-TIME HOMEBUYER AFFORDABILITY YEAR 1988

Starter Home Price	10% Down Payment	Loan Amount	Effective Interest Rate	Plus PMI	Monthly Payment	Qualifying Income
$76,650	$7,667	$69,003	9.31%	9.56%	$583	$27,995

Data source: National Association of Realtors

Transportation

Before you choose the kind of transportation you'll want or need, think about where you said you'd like to live. In some cities, it's quite easy to walk or use public transportation. In some places, a vehicle is almost a necessity. Consider, too, your physical condition and your mechanical ability.

Do you want to get around by:

☐ Walking

☐ Bicycle

☐ Motorcycle

☐ Public transportation

☐ Other

☐ Your own car, previously owned

☐ Your own car, bought new every 7-8 years

☐ Your own car, bought new every 3-4 years

☐ Your own car, bought new every year

If you want to own your own car:

What make _____ Model _____ Year _____

How many miles per month do you plan to drive? _____

Monthly car payments $ _____

Gasoline $ _____

Maintenance and insurance $ _____

Public transportation $ _____

Transportation $ _____ [2]

Enter at [2] on page 92.

NEW CAR PRICES Year 1988		
Domestic	Import	Average
$14,008	$15,316	$14,387

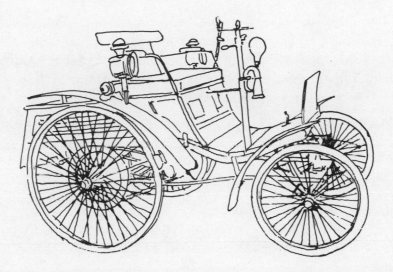

PASSENGER CAR OPERATING COSTS
Year 1989

Variable Costs in Cents per Mile				Cost per 10,000 Miles			
Gas & Oil	Maintenance	Tires	Variable Total	Fixed Cost	Cost	Total Cost	Cost Per Mile
$.052	$.019	$.008	$.079	$790.00	$3,030	$3,820	$.382

Costs include Insurance, License and Registration, Depreciation, Finance Charge.
Source: *Family Economics Review*

Clothing

Your clothing budget depends on your talents, your tastes, and the time you want to devote to this part of your life. Perhaps you are one of those creative types who can whip up exciting outfits from plastic bags and old neckties. Maybe you always have and always will live in blue jeans. Bargain hunters, given enough time, can produce expensive designer wardrobes at discount store prices. Others wouldn't consider buying anything at less than full price. Some people, short on time, are willing to spend whatever is necessary to get what they need in a hurry.

Think about how much money you feel would be a reasonable amount to spend each year on clothing for yourself and each member of your family. How do you prefer to come by your clothes? Do you want or need an extensive wardrobe, or will just the basics do? Don't forget to make allotments for shoes, bathing suits, and other items that may not come immediately to mind. Then answer the questions below.

For clothing, I plan to:

☐ Sew for the family

☐ Purchase recycled clothing

☐ Buy from discount or economy catalogs and stores

☐ Always buy on sale

☐ Buy from department stores and boutiques

☐ Buy designer fashions

☐ Other _____

I would like to have:

☐ A minimum wardrobe

☐ A moderate-size wardrobe

☐ An extensive wardrobe

☐ What I want, when I want it

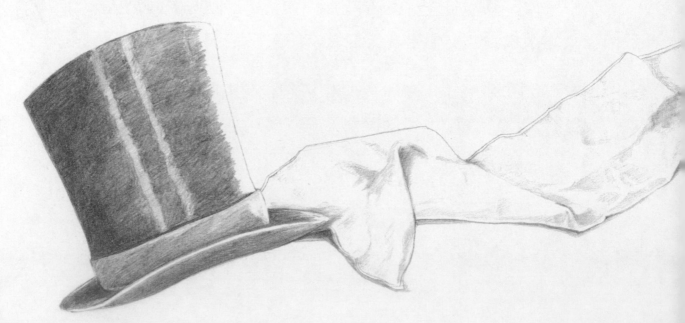

List each member of your family and his or her projected yearly clothing budget:

Family Member   Annual Budget

_____ $ _____

_____ $ _____

_____ $ _____

_____ $ _____

_____ $ _____

_____ $ _____

          Annual family total $ _____

Divide this figure by 12 to get your monthly clothing budget.

          Clothing $ _____ [3]

Enter at [3] on page 92.

Food

Some years back a TV commercial featured a well-known naturalist who asked that memorable question, "Ever eat a pine tree?" He went on to inform viewers that "Some parts *are* edible." Perhaps. But most of us have come to expect more sophisticated fare. Still, there's plenty of room for negotiation between grazing in the forest and living solely on steak and caviar. The government has defined three kinds of food plans, each of which supplies the necessary nutrients. The Thrifty Plan is based on low-cost foods (beans, rice) but these may be unappealing to some people and may take more time for preparation. The Moderate Plan offers a greater variety of foods. The Liberal Plan lets you buy whatever you want regardless of the cost.

Would you like your diet to be based on:

☐ Government surplus food   ☐ The Moderate Plan

☐ The low-cost Thrifty Plan   ☐ The Liberal Plan

Do you have any special dietary habits that might increase your food budge (i.e., gourmet cooking is your hobby, you have a restricted diet)? The chart on page 85 may help you come up with an amount.

Food $ _____ [4]

Enter at [4] on page 92.

Sundries

Sundries are all those little things you pick up at the grocery or drug store: shampoo, deodorant, toilet paper, cleaning supplies, and the like. How much would you plan to spend on these items a month?

Sundries $ _____ [5]

Enter at [5] on page 92.

	Thrifty Plan	Low-Cost Plan	Moderate-Cost Plan	Liberal Plan
COST OF FOOD AT HOME Per month – August 1989				
FAMILIES				
Family of 2				
20–50 years	$195.90	$245.70	$303.50	$377.10
Family of 4				
Couple & 2				
preschoolers	284.90	353.30	431.90	530.30
Couple & 2				
school age	326.60	415.10	519.60	625.50
INDIVIDUALS				
Child:				
1-2 years	51.30	$62.10	72.40	87.30
3-5 years	55.50	$67.80	83.60	100.20
6-8 years	67.90	$89.70	112.30	130.80
9-11 years	80.60	$102.00	131.40	151.90
Male: 20–50				
years	93.60	118.90	148.90	180.20
Female: 20–50				
years	84.50	104.50	127.00	162.60

Source: *Family Economics Review*

Entertainment and Recreation

Although the following budget items are not necessary to sustain life, they *do* have an impact on your self-esteem and life satisfaction. Answer the following questions, remembering to consider your spouse and your children's needs as well.

Monthly Total

How many times/month will you eat at a restaurant? _____

    What will your average bill be? $ _____

        How much per month will be spent on meals out? $ _____

Would you like to entertain friends?

        What would you spend per month? $ _____

Would you like to attend concerts, movies, theaters, sports events, and the like?

        What would you spend per month? $ _____

Will you buy books or tapes? Subscribe to newspapers and magazines?

        How much a month would you like to spend? $ _____

Will you have hobbies or take part in sports that cost money?

What? _____

        How much will you need a month? $ _____

If you have children, what kinds of recreational/educational opportunities do you want for them? (Check their ages again.)

What? _____

        How much will be spent per month? $ _____

One more consideration: Do you want to have special equipment related to entertainment or recreation? Would you like to have a stereo or CD player, VCR, musical instruments, boat, plane, country club, or health club membership?

What do you want to spend on them per month? $ _____

        Total entertainment $ _____ [6]

Enter at [6] on page 92.

Vacations

This is not so much a "whether or not" budget item as it is a "where and how often" expenditure. It's been shown that taking time off is an important part of maintaining good physical and mental health. How do you want to do it?

Do you want to take a vacation:

☐ Monthly
☐ Every six months
☐ Yearly

☐ Every two years
☐ Every three to five years
☐ Other _____

What kind of vacation would you like to be able to afford:

☐ Car trip to relatives
☐ Camping/hiking
☐ Day trips to local amusements
☐ A week at the seashore or mountain cabin
☐ Car trips to places of interest

☐ Plane trips to places of interest
☐ Foreign travel
☐ Cruises, travel packages, or exotic clubs
☐ Other _____
☐ Other _____

What will you want to budget every year to meet your vacation objectives? $ _____

Divide that figure by 12 to come up with your monthly figure.

Vacation $ _____ [7]

Enter at [7] on page 92.

Child Care

If both parents are working while there are young children in the family (a reasonable assumption), you will need to consider your child care options. First, look back to see how many children you are planning to have and their ages.

Would you have:

☐ No need for child care

☐ A relative to care for them

☐ A cooperative arrangement with a relative or friend

☐ Care in a community-based center

☐ A private nursery school or day care center

☐ A sitter coming into your home

☐ Live-in help

NATIONAL AVERAGE FOR CHILD CARE COSTS		
	Housekeeper	Day care center
Infants & toddlers	$3.67/hour	$2.45/hour
Preschoolers	$3.14/hour	$1.94/hour

Source: *American Demographics*, Feb. 1989

How much will this cost per child, per month?

child one $ _____

child two $ _____

child three $ _____

Total child care costs $ _____ [8]

Enter at [8] on page 92.

DEPENDENT CARE

If you indicated at the beginning of this exercise that you plan to care for a dependent other than your children (a parent or grandparent, for example), remember to add that into your monthly budget. What do you plan to spend on dependent care? $ _____

What if there is a divorce or separation in your future? Will you need to pay alimony or child support? How much? $ _____ Keep these costs in mind as you plan for monthly reserves.

Health Care

Because an unforeseen accident or illness can play havoc with the most carefully planned budget, health insurance is a must. Many employers will subsidize your health insurance, but you usually will have to pay a portion of the cost. What kind of care do you want?

☐ Government-subsidized free clinics   ☐ Private physician and dentist

☐ Health maintenance organization care

See page 94 for some sample annual costs. Divide your projected annual cost by 12 months.

Health care $ _____ [9]

Enter at [9] on page 92.

Furnishings

You probably need to purchase replacement equipment and items for your home such as linens, appliances, furniture and decorative items. Assume you have most of these items by this time.

Annual budget $ _____ divided by 12

Furnishings $ _____ [10]

Enter at [10] on page 92.

Savings

This is an important part of any budget. There are predictable things to save for (a house, new furnishings, children's college, retirement) as well as things you'd rather not think about (losing your job, a major illness). Spending money on a new roof or water heater isn't fun, but sometimes it has to be done. And it's a lot easier if you've planned for it. As a rule of thumb, every family should save at least six months' income in case of emergency.

What do you feel you should save each month for:

☐ Emergencies   ☐ Retirement

☐ Repairs, replacements, or major purchases   ☐ Income cushion

☐ Children's college

Savings $ _____ [11]

Enter at [11] on page 92.

Miscellaneous

Are there things important to you that we haven't mentioned yet? Think about your values. Here are some possible additional expenses. Add your own if you need to.

What will be your yearly budget for holiday gifts and birthdays?

per month $ _____

Will you have pets? If so, what kind? _____

How much per month will it cost to keep them?

$ _____

Will you make contributions to social, political, or religious organizations? If so, how much per month?

$ _____

Do you want to send your children to private schools?   Yes   No   Undecided

How much will this cost per month? $ _____

Other costs, list:

_____ $ _____

_____ $ _____

_____ $ _____

Miscellaneous $ _____ [12]

Enter at [12] on page 92.

ESTIMATED COST OF RAISING A CHILD
Urban children, birth to 18 years old

Moderate-Cost Level, June 1989

Midwest	$105,055
Northeast	110,891
South	114,483
West	116,995

Source: *Family Economics Review*

If you save $100 per month at 8% interest, you will have in:

5 years	$7,397
10 years	18,417
15 years	34,835
20 years	59,295

AVERAGE ANNUAL COLLEGE COSTS
by type of institution (1985-86)

	Public 4-Year	Private 4-Year	Public 2-Year	Private 2-Year
Tuition	$1,242	$5,418	$659	$3,719
Room & board	2,473	2,781	1,180	2,591
Books & supplies	373	384	355	$367
Personal & Transportation	1,226	1,076	1,433	1,018
Total	5,314	9,659	3,627	7,695

Source: College Board Data

Your Budget Profile

Here's the moment of truth. Go through the exercise again and enter the monthly amounts you indicated in each category in the appropriate space below. Then add the column to come up with your total monthly budget.

[1] Housing $ _____

[2] Transportation $ _____

[3] Clothing $ _____

[4] Food $ _____

[5] Sundries $ _____

[6] Entertainment $ _____

[7] Vacations $ _____

[8] Child care $ _____

[9] Health care $ _____

[10] Furnishings $ _____

[11] Savings $ _____

[12] Miscellaneous $ _____

Total: $ _____

What Salary Will Support this Lifestyle?

The figure you have just computed is the total amount of money you will need to bring home in your paycheck. But you will need to earn more money than this figure because of deductions from you paycheck for Social Security, state and federal taxes.

So before you begin looking for a career, you need to figure the gross pay (salary) needed to meet your budget requirements.

Taxing authorities have charts for factoring precise figures. For the sake of this exercise, figure an average of 20% is withheld from your paycheck. What you have left after taxes have been witheld is called net pay or takehome pay. This is the amount of money you have left to cover your expenses.

To find the monthly salary you will need to cover your expenses, divide your monthly expenses by 80 percent.

Expenses (or net pay) divided by 80% = Gross pay

_____ 80% = _____
　　　　total from page 92　　　　　　　　　　your required monthly salary

Multiply this figure by 12 (months) to get the annual salary figure required.

_____ X 12 = _____
　　your required monthly salary　　　　　　　your required annual salary

Keep this figure in mind as you start researching career possiblities. You might start by reading the employment section of classified advertisements in both your local newspaper and the newspaper of the closest large city. Do the jobs that meet your financial needs sound interesting?

AVERAGE ANNUAL EXPENDITURES

	One Person	Two Persons	Three Persons	Four Persons	Five Persons	Six or More Persons
EXPENSES:						
Food	$1,834	$3,402	$3,947	$4,740	$5,202	$5,759
Food at home	874	1,898	2,373	2,848	3,344	3,854
Food away from home	960	1,504	1,574	1,892	1,858	1,905
Housing	4,632	7,403	8,356	,829	8,858	9,250
Utilities, fuels	1,008	1,683	1,908	2,129	2,115	2,278
Household operations	167	292	485	614	481	446
Housekeeping supplies	164	328	375	438	426	454
Household furnishings	485	1,113	1,204	1,359	1,212	1,304
Clothing	731	1,264	1,647	1,945	1,873	2,095
Transportation	2,394	5,036	6,082	6,721	6,319	6,469
Health Care	764	1,328	1,213	1,284	1,284	1,257
Entertainment	611	1,150	1,416	1,626	1,603	1,379
Personal care products and services	175	320	361	381	396	424
Miscellaneous	336	541	570	761	603	507
Cash contributions	551	1,047	761	621	556	644
Personal insurance and pensions	991	2,272	2,654	3,136	2,714	2,331
INCOME:						
Money before taxes	14,291	26,659	29,511	35,744	31,865	29,734
Personal taxes	1,467	2,697	2,521	2,996	2,151	1,736
Money after taxes	12,823	23,962	26,900	32,749	29,714	27,997

This table is to assist with sample expenditures for previous budget exercises.
Columns do not total because there are various small incidental expenses not listed.

Source: *Comsumer Expenditure Survey: Integrated Survey Data,* 1984-86.
U.S. Department of Labor, Bureau of Labor Statistics. August 1989. Bulletin 2333

In Over Your Head?

As much as we would sometimes like to ignore them, numbers don't lie. You may be surprised at many of the costs. If your budget total seems unreasonably high, you will need to make some adjustments.

Go back and review your figures. Where could you make cuts most easily? Write your adjusted figures in a different color pen or pencil. These numbers should add up to the minimum amount of money you need to lead a lifestyle that would be acceptable to you.

Roberta, for example, decided that the several hundred dollars a month she could save by giving up her luxury dreamcar for a more modest vehicle wouldn't really be painful. It may be depressing to adjust your dreams downward, but being a slave to your lifestyle isn't fun, either.

Bob and Barbara, like many people, found themselves "house poor." They dreamed of having a big new house in the best part of town. And they built it. But the mortgage payments are so high that no money is left for little pleasures like an occasional dinner and movie in town. Several years of living in anxiety because of their overstretched budget have taken a toll on their health, their marriage, and their life satisfaction.

When Jason lost his job, he decided to get a roommate to share expenses. He found he could make ends meet by cutting out most recreational expenses and adjusting his eating habits: no steak for a while, lots of spaghetti.

Back to your budget. Did the figure you arrived at on page 92 seem higher than the salary you're likely to earn on your own? What amount do you think you could reasonably expect to earn? Write that figure on line b below. Next determine your net income (line a), if you earn that salary (see formula page 93). Now reallocate your funds. Write the adjusted figures for your hard times budget below. The total should be a figure no larger than your *own* income. Don't count on your phantom spouse here.

HARD TIMES BUDGET

1.	Housing	$ _____
2.	Transportation	$ _____
3.	Clothing	$ _____
4.	Food	$ _____
5.	Sundries	$ _____
6.	Entertainment	$ _____
7.	Vacations	$ _____
8.	Child care	$ _____
9.	Health care	$ _____
10.	Furnishings	$ _____
11.	Savings	$ _____
12.	Miscellaneous	$ _____
	a) Total:	$ _____
	b) Gross monthly salary	$ _____

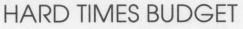

Some Sample Budgets

Phyllis, a single mother of two, teaches English at a high school in Southern California. Her sons are twelve and ten years old. The family lives in a small house in one of the older sections of town. It's a long drive to work for Phyllis, but new housing is very expensive. Besides, they like their old neighborhood. The boys attend a magnet school where they are getting an early chance to excel at languages and math. Every Friday night, the whole family goes out for pizza. Phyllis's hobby is photography. She and several other amateur photographers share a darkroom. Every summer, the family takes a two-week car trip to somewhere Phyllis can take photos and the boys can enjoy and learn from.

HER BUDGET

1. Housing	$	650
2. Transportation	$	225
3. Clothing	$	140
4. Food	$	325
5. Sundries	$	30
6. Entertainment	$	40
7. Vacations	$	55
8. Child care	$	25
9. Health care	$	125
10. Furnishings	$	30
11. Savings	$	100
12. Miscellaneous	$	55
Total:	$	1,800

What is the gross monthly income required to come up with this net? $ _____

Will has been in the army for three years. The pay's not great, but since he's single and doesn't have to pay for room or board, he has no complaints. Will loves to travel— that's one reason he enlisted. He saves part of every check for his travel fund in order to take advantage of the special prices he can get while he's in the service. Last year he spent a month in Europe. This year he wants to go to Japan. Will recently opened another savings account to save money for a new car.

HIS BUDGET

1.	Housing	$	_____
2.	Transportation	$	_____
3.	Clothing	$	_____
4.	Food	$	_____
5.	Sundries	$	_____
6.	Entertainment	$	_____
7.	Vacations	$	_____
8.	Child care	$	_____
9.	Health care	$	_____
10.	Furnishings	$	_____
11.	Savings	$	_____
12.	Miscellaneous	$	_____
	Total:	$	$550

What is the gross monthly income required to come up

with this net? $ _____

Jeff and Francie and their two kids live in a new housing development in Indiana. Jeff works at a nearby factory, where he's been employed for 15 years. Francie works in the office at the plant. The twins are 14. They're bright kids, and Jeff and Francie want to send them to college. They were worried a few years ago when many people at the factory were laid off, but Jeff and Francie both kept their jobs. The children's college fund is intact and growing. When the family goes on vacation, their main concern is getting out of the city. Usually, they go camping or rent a cabin on a lake. Francie says that's about the only time the whole family does anything together anymore — the boys are busy with part-time jobs and afterschool activities. But she and Jeff have started going out alone a couple times a month, something they both enjoy.

THEIR BUDGET

1. Housing	$	_____
2. Transportation	$	_____
3. Clothing	$	_____
4. Food	$	_____
5. Sundries	$	_____
6. Entertainment	$	_____
7. Vacations	$	_____
8. Child care	$	_____
9. Health care	$	_____
10. Furnishings	$	_____
11. Savings	$	_____
12. Miscellaneous	$	_____
Total:	$	$2,300

Total: $1,500/month take-home salary, Jeff

$800/month take-home salary, Francie

What is the gross monthly income required to come up with this net? $ _____

Carl is a psychiatrist and Ruth is a bank executive. They live with their small daughter in a cooperative apartment in New York City. Since their careers call for long and unpredictable hours at work, they have live-in help for the baby. They don't have a car — most of the time it's not necessary. They rent one when they need to. Vacations have been fewer since the baby was born, but the family is looking for a weekend home in the country. The full-time babysitter also makes it easier for Carl and Ruth to go out at night. They both love the theater and enjoy trying out new restaurants.

THEIR BUDGET

1. Housing $ _____

2. Transportation $ _____

3. Clothing $ _____

4. Food $ _____

5. Sundries $ _____

6. Entertainment $ _____

7. Vacations $ _____

8. Child care $ _____

9. Health care $ _____

10. Furnishings $ _____

11. Savings $ _____

12. Miscellaneous $ _____

                Total: $ _____ $5,000 _____

Total: $2,800/month take-home salary, Carl

$3,200/month take-home salary, Ruth

What is the gross monthly income required to come up with this net? $ _____

Ben is a golf pro in Fort Lauderdale. Lynn is a nurse, but she's been home full-time since the birth of their first child. The family has a ranch house in the suburbs with a big yard for the kids (now four and seven) and a garden for Lynn. They have two cars, neither of them new, but both kept in good condition by Ben. Outings are usually casual events like picnics at the beach. They like to have friends over for barbecue. Since Ben knows golf pros all over the country, vacation time means swapping homes with another family — a different part of the country each year. This year they're all looking forward to a stay in Colorado.

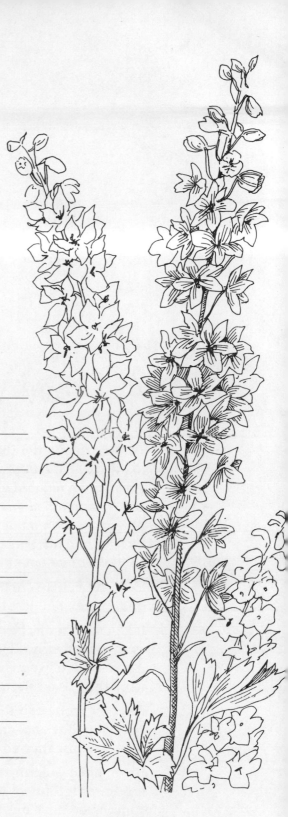

THEIR BUDGET

1. Housing $ _____

2. Transportation $ _____

3. Clothing $ _____

4. Food $ _____

5. Sundries $ _____

6. Entertainment $ _____

7. Vacations $ _____

8. Child care $ _____

9. Health care $ _____

10. Furnishings $ _____

11. Savings $ _____

12. Miscellaneous $ _____

Total: $ _____$2,300_____

Total: $2300/month take-home salary

What is the gross monthly income required to come up with this net? $ _____

A Few Words about Poverty

Though the United States is one of the richest nations on earth, millions of its citizens today are living in poverty. Many of these are homeless, living in shelters or on the street, often reduced to begging for quarters or going through garbage cans in order to eat. For many others, a majority of them women, children, and the elderly, life offers little more than anxiety about paying the rent or buying the groceries they need. The societal and historical forces that have caused this situation must be changed, but that will take time.

How can you assure that you will not be a future poverty statistic? There are no guarantees, but here are some things you might think about:

If you are female, be aware of the fact that, on average, women earn only 66 cents for every dollar earned by a man. Part of this discrepancy is due to discrimination. Part of it is a result of women clustering in career fields such as nursing, teaching, and clerical work that, as a rule, are not high paying.

Another problem is that, at least in middle-class white culture, women grow up believing that someone else will take care of them. They do not adequately prepare for a job because they do not believe that they will ever *have* to have one.

If you are a woman, and if you are still in school, one of the best things you can do to ensure your future is to take math and science classes, and do as well in them as you can. If you have any skills and interests related to traditionally male careers, pursue them. Even though a woman engineer may not earn as much as a male engineer, she almost certainly will make more than a bookkeeper or secretary.

Assume that you *will* have to support yourself. Plan for that eventuality and, if it comes about, at least you will be prepared.

Could You Become a Poverty Statistic?

In 1987, 32,546,000 people in the United States lived below the poverty level. That is 13.5 percent of the total population.

Twelve percent of all families live below the poverty level.

Nearly 20 percent of all families with children are headed by a woman.

54.7 percent Of all families with children under 18, headed by a woman with no husband present, live below the poverty level.

In the United States, 21.2 percent of all children live below the poverty level.

Families maintained by men have median weekly earnings of $478. Families maintained by women have median weekly earnings of $317. Married-couple families where both are earners have median weekly earnings of $741.

What do you think contributes to poverty in this country?

_____

_____

_____

What might cause you to become one of these statistics?

_____

_____

How can you prevent that from happening?

_____

_____

_____

_____

Source: U.S. Department of Commerce, Bureau of the Census, Current Population Reports, October 1988.

Money Isn't Everything

On the other hand, it's quite possible to put more emphasis on money than it deserves: if only we were rich and famous, we think, we'd certainly be happy. But would we? Every day, it seems, there is news of one more celebrity getting divorced, being treated for drug addiction or alcoholism or emotional illness, or even committing suicide.

We won't attempt to say why this is so. But the stories do demonstrate that wealth and fame do not guarantee a rewarding life. Status symbols — the cars, houses, jewelry, and so on — are very effective at making other people envious, but they often mean little to their owners.

Studies have shown that people with a comfortable income are usually much happier than those living in poverty. But excessive amounts of money do not seem to add significantly to life satisfaction.

Many people make conscious decisions to forgo higher incomes in order to do something they think is more worthwhile, such as teaching. Besides their service to society, teachers value other benefits such as the vacation time to pursue other interests or be with their families.

A well-paid advertising executive who really wants to write short stories may be less satisfied with her life than a bus driver who loves his job. That is why it is so important to consider your values when making career decisions. Go back to the values exercise on page 35 and review the values that are most important to you. Whatever course you take in life should be compatible with them.

Every job has psychological and emotional costs. The trick is to find a balance: that is, a job that pays enough to support the kind of *physical* lifestyle you want, while not draining your *spirit* by forcing you to deny the values you hold most dear.

Consider the following stories. What values are being sacrificed in each case? We've used Bert's story as an example.

(You will recall that our values categories are adventure, family, knowledge and truth, power, personal integrity and moral courage, money or wealth, friendship and companionship, recognition, independence and freedom, security, beauty or aesthetics, creativity, and helping others.)

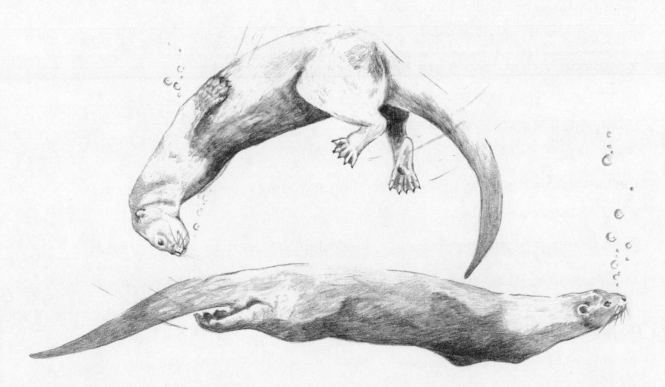

BERT'S STORY

I've wanted to be a missionary ever since I was a boy. Every year, people would come to our church from some distant country and show slides and talk about the work they were doing for the people there. I love to travel, and my religion has always been important to me. Right now, I'm stationed on an island in the South Pacific. We're building a new school and a much-needed hospital. But it's taking longer than it should because sometimes the money doesn't come through. It's difficult when your only support comes from people who are thousands of miles away. I have to remind myself to have faith and that, so far, things have always worked out. The people here are wonderful, and they've taught me so much. But I never thought I could be so thrilled about getting a bar of soap or a box of chocolate in the mail. Last time I was home, I went into a supermarket and just stared at all the variety — the sheer number of things you can just pick up and buy. They even carry it to your car for you! But that was three years ago. I haven't seen my family since then. I'm not sure when I'll be sent somewhere else, and that makes it hard. But I think we've really accomplished something for the people on this island, and that makes it all worthwhile.

What are the sacrifices Bert has made?

Time away from his family, little access to material goods, dependence on others
for support, lack of control over his own future

Which values do those sacrifices reflect?

Family, money and wealth, security

What are his rewards?

Feeling that he's making a difference, being surrounded by people he respects

Which values do they reflect?

Personal integrity and moral courage, friendship and companionship, helping
others

Do you share some of Bert's values?   Yes   No   Undecided

Are you willing to make similar sacrifices?   Yes   No   Undecided

If so, you may be happy with a career like Bert's.

LEON'S STORY

All I have to do to remind myself of the power I hold is to walk through the halls of this company. Five thousand employees, and they all know I could promote them or give them a raise — or fire them on the spot. I like the way everyone smiles and calls me "sir" and goes out of the way to try to please me. I guess it sounds as though I'm just on a power trip, but I've worked hard to build this company and earn the respect of the people who work here. When I think of all the years of 60 or 80 hours a week in the office, all the kids' birthday parties I missed, the anniversaries I forgot . . . . Well, maybe it's no wonder that I don't get the same respect at home that I do at work. The kids are grown now, and I feel that I hardly know them. My wife has built a life of her own, and I'm not exactly indispensable to her. But I love the job. I plan to stay here as long as my health holds out — maybe until I'm 75.

What are the sacrifices Leon has made?

_____

Which values do these sacrifices reflect?

_____

What are Leon's rewards?

_____

Which values do they reflect?

_____

Do you share Leon's values?   Yes   No   Undecided

Are you willing to make similar sacrifices?   Yes   No   Undecided

If so, you might be happy with a similar career.

VINCENT'S STORY

Yesterday I sold my first painting. You might think that after all those years when no one was interested, selling one painting wouldn't mean very much. But you would be wrong. It's not the recognition or the money I'm after. I see such incredible beauty in the world, and I only want to find a way to express it and share it. I've had to take many jobs over the years — cab driver, hospital orderly, janitor — but I've never thought of myself as anything but an artist.

What are the sacrifices Vincent has made?

_____

_____

Which values do they reflect?

_____

_____

What are Vincent's rewards?

_____

_____

Which values do they reflect?

_____

_____

Do you share Vincent's values?   Yes   No   Undecided

Would you be ready to make similar sacrifices?

                                         Yes   No   Undecided

If so, you might be happy with a similar career.

SARA'S STORY

Being an environmental scientist is one of the most important jobs I can think of. After all, this is the only planet we have. I really love my job and I don't take the responsibility lightly. I had no social life in school because I was so serious about my studies. But, truthfully, I've always preferred books to parties. The thing is, I'm still studying. There's always something new to learn. I hardly ever see anyone away from work. I can't remember the last time I went shopping or played a round of golf. I've always wanted to have children, but that plan is on hold for now. Last week, though, we learned that fish have returned to a river I helped clean up and — well, you don't get a feeling like that from an afternoon of shopping. It's not easy, but I'm proud of what I do.

What sacrifices has Sara had to make? _____

_____

_____

What values categories would you put them under?

_____

_____

List Sara's rewards. _____

_____

_____

To which values categories do they belong? _____

_____

Do you and Sara have similar values?   Yes   No   Undecided

Would you be willing to make the same sacrifices?

                          Yes   No   Undecided

If so, this might be a career for you to think about.

ROSE'S STORY

I've always had two goals: to have a good family life, and to be successful at a career. I love to travel, and for a while I thought I might be a pilot. But that would mean being away from home a lot. I'm pretty good at math, too, and I'm a stickler for details, so I decided to become an accountant. I worked for a big firm for a few years, until Allen and I decided to start a family. Then I opened my own office at home. It's not as prestigious, but since I can control the number of clients I take on I was able to scale the job down when the children were small and spend most of my time with them. Now that they're in school all day, I work full-time. I'm the boss, though, so I can arrange my schedule in order to be there for special events at school or when somebody's home sick. Allen has a good job, too, but it's important to me to know that I could support the family on my own if I had to.

What sacrifices has Rose made for her career? _____

_____

What values categories would you place them in? _____

_____

What are her rewards? _____

_____

What values do you think they mirror? _____

_____

Are your values similar to Rose's?   Yes   No   Undecided

Would you make the same sacrifices?   Yes   No   Undecided

If so, a career like hers might make you happy.

You Win Some, You Lose Some

Every job has its rewards and its sacrifices. How well a given career could work for you depends on your own values. It's important to recognize which values are compatible with a job and which are not. See how adept you are at recognizing which traits a job will call forth, and which it will deny. For each of the following careers, list the values you think will be rewarded and those that will most likely be sacrificed.

Soldier
Rewards: _Adventure_
Sacrifices: _Freedom, creativity_

Computer programmer
Rewards: _Security, creativity_
Sacrifices: _Beauty and aesthetics, adventure_

Professional athlete
Rewards: _Recognition, power, adventure_
Sacrifices: _Freedom, security_

Fire fighter
Rewards: _____
Sacrifices: _____

Veterinarian
Rewards: _____
Sacrifices: _____

Fashion model
Rewards: _____
Sacrifices: _____

Radio Announcer
Rewards: _____
Sacrifices: _____

Social worker
Rewards: _____
Sacrifices: _____

Mechanic
Rewards: _____
Sacrifices: _____

Farmer
Rewards: _____
Sacrifices: _____

Truck driver
Rewards: _____
Sacrifices: _____

Flight attendant
Rewards: _____
Sacrifices: _____

Homemaker
Rewards: _____
Sacrifices: _____

Garbage hauler
Rewards: _____
Sacrifices: _____

Accountant
Rewards: _____
Sacrifices: _____

Resort owner
Rewards: _____
Sacrifices: _____

Perhaps you found it difficult to determine which values the preceding jobs would not satisfy. There are several possible explanations, if you did. First of all, we generally look only at the rewards (financial and emotional) a given career has to offer. Personal and spiritual sacrifices are seldom mentioned, if they are even perceived. Also, some sacrifices are not apparent immediately. In some cases, they may not appear at all. Anything from your individual employer to the economic situation of the world can affect the way you feel about your job.

Many people end up in careers they've trained for, but find that their careers don't satisfy all their values. What can you do about that? Well, you can always change jobs. But sometimes there are powerful reasons to stay put. For example, a college professor who has invested many years in education may well hesitate before chucking it all to become a dancer just because teaching doesn't satisfy her creative side. Sometimes the job market is so bleak that anyone with any kind of job feels lucky. Or, if you have three children to support, you may have to pass on what could be your last chance to play minor league baseball at the minimum wage.

Does that mean you're doomed to a lifetime of misery or, at best, of vague dissatisfaction? Not at all. Work may represent a sizable chunk of your life, but it has no claim on your free time. Many people have found after-hours activities that fill in and make amends for those things that are lacking from 9 to 5.

Daniel is a garbage hauler. His top values are security and power. The job pays well, and it is certainly secure. ("One thing we know for sure," his boss is fond of saying, "there will always be garbage.") But power? Not much evidence of that. One day while Daniel was teaching his daughter how to throw a fast ball, a neighbor stopped by, watched a while, and suggested that Daniel might make a good Little League coach. He knew of a team that needed one. Daniel said, "why not," and, he's been having a great time leading his team to glory ever since.

Maria, for example, is an electrical engineer. Her top values are security, recognition, and aesthetics. Engineering meets her needs for security, but didn't satisfy her other requirements. She didn't want to give up her job, but she needed more satisfaction in her life. So she joined a community theater group. She loves the atmosphere, she loves the plays, and, most of all, she loves the applause.

Rodrigo is the executive director of a youth-service agency. Security and helping others are his top values. The job was great — he didn't want to leave it — but the pay was low and unlikely to improve. He couldn't save any money, and that made him feel insecure. When he received a small windfall from his grandmother, he decided to put it to work. He studied about investments and real estate, found some friends interested in a joint venture, and made some long-term plans. By investing wisely, he was able to develop an account for his retirement or for financial emergencies that might occur.

On each of the following lines, you'll find an occupation followed by a list of values. Circle those values you think would be met by the career. Then, on the line provided, state what this person might do to meet the other need.

Social worker: helping others   creativity   power _____

Assembly line worker: helping others   security   friendship _____

Carpenter: adventure   beauty and aesthetics   family _____

Sales representative: family   money   friendship _____

Homemaker: family   helping others   power _____

Museum guide: beauty and aesthetics   adventure   creativity _____

Professor: knowledge   creativity   recognition _____

Farmer: family   helping others   friendship _____

Psychologist: adventure   helping others   beauty and aesthetics _____

Accountant: power   money   creativity _____

Chemist: knowledge   creativity   recognition _____

Writer: creativity   helping others   friendship _____

Veterinarian: helping others   knowledge   power _____

Commitment

In high school, David, Michael, and Diane were inseparable. They agreed that music was the most important thing in the world. All were gifted musicians. The threesome could always be found in the music room at school, at the record store, or at the back stage entrance to Orchestra Hall. They loved all kinds of music — rock, jazz, classical, country, new age. And all vowed that, somehow, music would always be at the center of their lives.

After graduation, David attended a college with one of the best music programs in the country. Because of his excellent work there, he was awarded a fellowship to continue his studies in Europe. His dedication to his art eventually led to a job with one of the most prestigious orchestras in the United States.

Diane took a different track. While in college, she began singing with a local rock group. She and one of the other musicians started writing songs together. The rest of the group eventually fell apart, but Diane and her partner formed and reformed the band, playing anywhere they could get a job, sometimes without pay. They spent years auditioning, making demonstration records, trying to get noticed, and — most of all — working to improve their music. The band recently signed with an agent, and Diane hopes they will have a recording contract soon.

Michael didn't see much point in continuing his education after high school. Convinced that he would be the next country music superstar, he headed directly to Nashville and tried very hard — for about a week — to get discovered. Well, he thought, maybe he'd rather be a songwriter. He dashed off two sets of lyrics and sent them to his favorite singer. When there was no response, Michael got angry. "Who wants to be part of an arrogant industry like this anyway," he reassured himself as he tried to hitch a ride home. He'd be much happier working for his uncle's construction company, a place where he'd surely be appreciated.

As the above story demonstrates, ability alone will not make you successful. In the end, whether or not you *can* do something may be less important than how much you *want* to do it, how committed you are to achieving your goal.

Lots of people have dreams. But, like Michael, many people are unwilling to put in the necessary work to make their dreams come true. David and Diane did not succeed through luck, but through persistence and hard work. What kind of persistence would it take to realize *your* dream?

While most jobs require some kind of commitment toward training or education, the amount varies. You can probably get a beginning clerical position with only a high school business class. To be a psychiatrist, however, you have to go through college and medical school before you even *begin* your psychiatric training. That's quite a commitment — of time, energy, and money.

Similarly, some careers require continued commitment. It may be possible to be a casual or part-time sales clerk, but it is difficult to imagine an uncommitted professional tennis player or member of Congress.

Often, the financial dividends and independence make the investment of time and effort worthwhile. Professionals like doctors and lawyers are among the highest paid people in our society. In most careers, the person who is most committed to the work — the one who has taken time to learn more or perform better — is the one likely to reach the top.

But there are no guarantees. Dancers and musicians, for example, may train for many years and still never earn a living from their art. They "do it for love," realizing that the odds are against them.

Before choosing your career, it's important to consider the degree of commitment you feel comfortable with — both in training and on-the-job performance. Some people want their work to be a dominant force in their lives. For others, it is important to have plenty of time for family and other interests.

Again, there is no right or wrong answer. The choice is yours. The following exercise will give you a better idea how an investment of time and/or money relates to future dividends.

An Investment in Education . . .

An investment in your future begins with education: the amount of time you are willing to devote to your training, the kinds of classes you are willing to take, and the amount of work you are willing to do in those classes. If you take math and science courses in high school (and do well in them), you will have more options concerning where you will go to college and what you will major in once you get there. Reading and writing skills are also essential in most career fields. College, of course, means more time committed. But, in general, time devoted to education will pay off in the long run.

The following chart demonstrates the relationship between time commitment and financial reward.

JOB TITLE	AVERAGE ANNUAL EARNINGS (1986)	POST HIGH SCHOOL TRAINING
Bricklayer	$21,320	144 hours classroom 3-year apprenticeship
Stenographer	21,700	2 years
Respiratory Therapist	22,300	1-year certificate or 4-year bachlors degree
Paramedic	24,300	nine months 216 hours classroom
Plumber	24,440	5-years apprenticeship
Elementary School Teacher	24,762	5 years
Computer Service Technician	26,700	2 years
Computer Systems Analyst	32,800	4 years
Air Traffic Controller	37,400	4 - 8 years school and experience
School Psychologist	37,600	7 - 9 years
Engineer	42,677	4+ years
College Professor	45,500	7 - 8 years
Chiropractor	55,000	6 - 8 years
Dentist	59,000	8 - 10 years
Attorney private practice	101,000	8 years
Physician	106,300	10 - 12 years

Earnings are for national average of mid career position.

. . . Yields Dividends for a Lifetime

While it may not seem that $10,000 or $20,000 per year increase in earning capability is a big enough of an inducement to spend between 3 and 10 more years in school or in training, let's look at what that extra effort can mean over a live time.

The chart below shows more dramatically how each year of education affects future earnings.

How many years do you plan to work between the age of 18 and 65?

_____ years in workforce

Multiply the number of years you plan to be in the workforce with each of the annual salaries listed below to find out how much you would earn over the course of your working life

$10,000 x _____ years in workforce = $ _____ lifetime earnings

$15,000 x _____ years in workforce = $ _____ lifetime earnings

$20,000 x _____ years in workforce = $ _____ lifetime earnings

$30,000 x _____ years in workforce = $ _____ lifetime earnings

$50,000 x _____ years in workforce = $ _____ lifetime earnings

What is the difference between a $10,000 and $15,000 annual salary

over a lifetime? $ _____

What is the difference between a $10,000 and $20,000 annual salary

over a lifetime? $ _____

What is the difference between a $10,000 and $30,000 annual salary

over a lifetime? $ _____

What is the difference between a $10,000 and $50,000 annual salary

over a lifetime? $ _____

75

70

Maybe the amount of education or training required for a job tht interests you still seems too long, higher income or no. Let's look at it another way.

65

The bar graph below represents an average lifespan — about 78 years. We've already filled it in for a high school graduate. That leaves you about 60 years to play around with. How will you spend that time?

60

55

Think about the kind of life you'd like to have, the job that appeals to you most, no matter how long the training required. Using the following questions as a guide, fill in the graph.

50

45

Using *polka dots* fill in and label the block of time for *post-high school training*.

40

35

Using *horizontal stripes* fill in and label the block(s) of time for *working full-time* and diagonal lines for *working part-time*.

30

Using *stars* fill in and label the block(s) of *time* for *outside the workforce* for raising a family or retirement.

25

20

High School

15

Junior High School

10

Elementary School

5

Use the information from your graph to answer the following questions.

How many years of post-high school training will you complete?

_____ years = a

How many years do you think you will work outside the home full-time?

_____ years = b

How many years do you think you will work outside the home part-time?

_____ years = c

Here are some interesting facts about your worklife.

How many hours might you work in your lifetime?

full-time   2,080 hours/year x _____ (b) = _____ f

part-time   1,000 hours/year x _____ (c) = _____ g

f _____ + g _____ = _____ hours you will work

in your lifetime.

That's a lot of time to be doing something that you do not find satisfying . . . that doesn't
correspond to your values or passions . . . that doesn't meet your lifestyle desires.

O.K. let's look at it one more way . . .

For every year of post-high school education, you will work _____ years.

Hint: $b + \dfrac{c}{a} =$ _____ h

Next time you think, 'Yuck, I can't stay in school _____ more years! I
didn't want to be a _____ anyway!' Remember these figures.
Education and training now are a small investment when you look at the long-range
payoffs in life satisfaction. Hang in there . . . you'll be glad you did!

Ask Someone Who's Been There

The information in this book is necessarily more general than we would like. To get some specific answers to the questions *you* have, interview three people over the age of 29. Use the following questions to help determine the rewards and sacrifices each person's job brings with it.

NAME _____

OCCUPATION _____

HOW LONG _____

How did you choose your occupation? _____
_____

Financially, does it let you live the way you prefer? _____
_____

If not, why not and what can you do about it? _____
_____

What rewards have you experienced? _____

   (Listen carefully here. Keep the different values categories in mind.)

   Values interpretation: _____

What sacrifices have you had to make for your career? _____

   Values interpretation: _____

What kind of commitment does this career require in terms of:

   Education _____

   Energy/endurance _____

   Stick-to-itiveness _____

If you had it to do over again, would you choose this career? _____

Why or why not? _____

Easier Said Than Done

As anyone who's ever vowed to lose weight or to save money knows, it's easier to *make* a commitment than it is to *keep* one. Long-term commitments are particularly hard to keep. In his book, *The Path of Least Resistance*, author Robert Fritz explains that, while it may be relatively easy to follow through at first, it is natural, over time, to fall back into comfortable old habits. Those who push on to meet their long-term goals or fulfill their dreams are usually those who have a clear vision of where they want to go or what they want to create.

By holding a picture in your mind of what it is you want, you will be better able to make the right decisions about your day-to-day actions. Should you study for the lit exam or go to the party? Well, what do you want? This is a key question, one you need to ask yourself often. It may be easier or more fun to go to the party. If you want to get into graduate school, however, you probably need to study for the test. Keeping your goal in mind will make it easier to decide.

Kay wants to save money for college. Her friend wants Kay to go with her on a ski vacation.

Jamal wants to do well at his weekend job. He feels like sleeping in on Saturday morning.

Lee wants to be in the school play. The thought of auditioning for a part makes him anxious.

Juanita wants to study art in France. Because of a scheduling problem, taking a French class would mean giving up her place in the school choir.

	It's easier to . . .	. . . than	But what I want is . . .	. . . therefore I will . . . .
Kay Jamal Lee Juanita You				

Complete this chart for Kay, Jamal, Lee, and Juanita.

What do you want? Look back to the goals you set in chapter 3 and fill in the chart above. Use this model to help make day-to-day decisions about realizing your dreams.

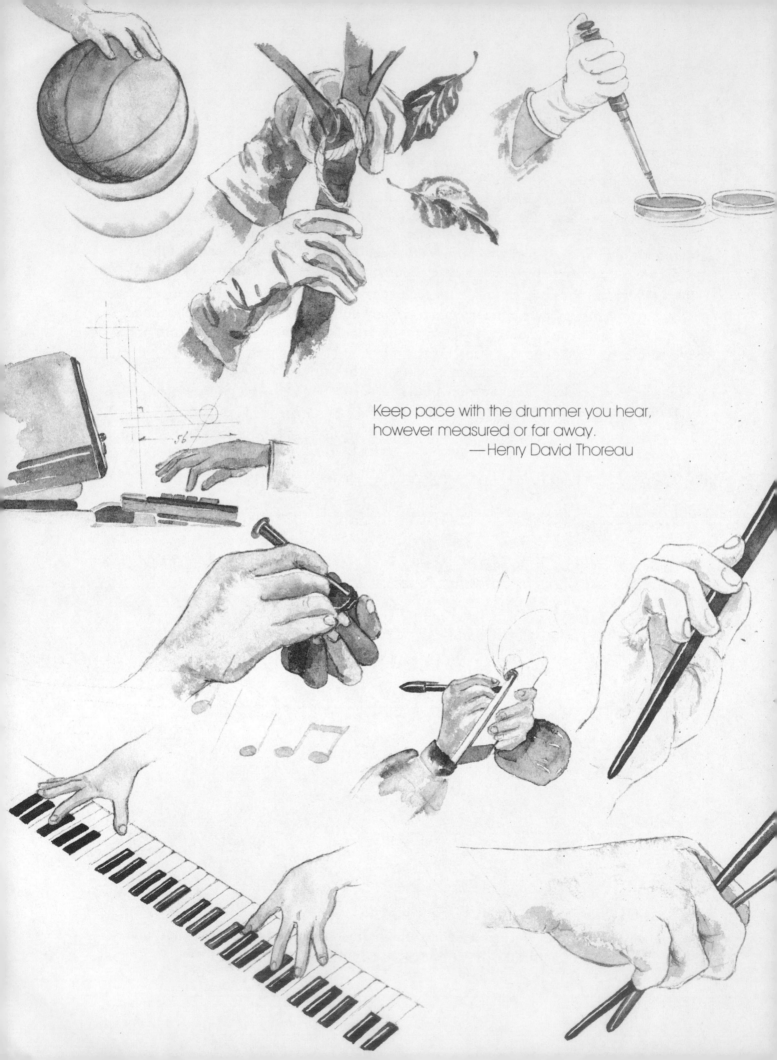

Keep pace with the drummer you hear,
however measured or far away.
—Henry David Thoreau

> I never did a day's work in my life – it was all fun.
>
> —Thomas Alva Edison

CHAPTER FIVE

Your Ideal Career

There's more to consider than just the work.

Section Two:
WHAT DO I WANT?

Gena was assigned to write a description of her ideal job for class. "I don't want you to tell me what the job is," Ms. Brown had instructed. "Just tell me where you'd like to work, who you'd like to work with, what you'd like to get from your job — things like that." Gena sat down at her desk, sharpened four pencils, chewed three sticks of gum, wrote a letter to her pen pal in Nova Scotia, filed her nails, and made serveral important phone calls. By 9 P.M. it was clear to her that she had no idea what to write.

A clever young woman, Gena decided to ask other people for their opinions. And they were more than happy to tell her what to do.

"A good job would involve a lot of travel," her friend Paul said. "You don't want to get stuck in some office all day, every day."

"It would have to be a job that lets you meet interesting people," her sister offered.

"I don't know about that," said her dad. "Be your own boss. That's the ticket."

"Do that and you'll never get a good night's sleep again," her grandfather proclaimed. "What you want is a secure job with a solid company. Something you know who can count on."

"If you want to have a family, it would help to have flexible hours," her mother said.

"Who cares about that?" asked her friend Susan. "I say go for the big bucks!"

Gena took her notes back to her desk. At first she didn't know what to make of such an odd assortment of opinions. As she thought about them, though, they began to make sense. A career, she realized, involves many things that have nothing at all to do with the actual work, yet greatly affect how effective and satisfied a worker will be.

In a way, Gena decided, choosing a rewarding career is like building a successful softball team. Every member of the team has an important role to play. Good pitching is essential, but without solid hitting and defense, it won't get you into the play-offs. Likewise, a job that pays well but is unrewarding in other respects won't make you happy.

What kinds of things should she consider in selecting a career? Gena looked back at the answers she'd collected and listed different categories. Traveling? That would involve the physical setting of a job, she decided. Working with interesting people seemed to relate to working conditions. Her father's comment about being her own boss, she felt, concerned relationships on the job. The security her grandfather urged on her related, she knew, to his values. Her mother was right — she definitely had to consider how her job would affect her family life. And, of course, there was the financial angle to consider.

Under each category, Gena listed the things that were most important to her. This was a good way to begin narrowing her career choices, she decided. And, if she used her imagination, she could come up with some new ideas, too. What jobs could she think of that would include as many elements from her list as possible? This just might be fun, she thought.

Before you start investigating specific careers, it's a good idea to think about the general characteristics you favor in a job. They can provide an outline that will make your career research much easier. If you know you want to live in the city, for example, you can cross "forest ranger" off your list of possible careers. Similarly, if you decide you want a job that lets you put family responsibilities first, you probably won't want to be a foreign correspondent for a network newscast.

On each of the following pages, you will find a brief description of a particular category of career considerations. A list of options involving that category follows. Check the box in front of any statement that appeals to you. Choose as many options as you like, but make sure they don't contradict each other. Feel free to add to the lists if we've overlooked something that appeals to you.

Physical Settings

By the setting of a job, we mean its geographic location as well as its specific working environment. Job satisfaction depends greatly on how you feel about where you work — and where your job forces you to live. You might love farming in the Midwest, for example. But if you have asthma or severe allergies, the humidity and pollen in the air could make your life miserable. Similarly, if you value beautiful surroundings, you probably won't want to work at a meat processing plant or a medical laboratory. And, if you can't stand to be indoors all day, a windowless inner office is not for you. Check the statements below that appeal to you.

- ☐ I would like to work in a city.
- ☐ I would like to work in the country.
- ☐ I would like to work in a small to medium-sized town.
- ☐ I would like to work in _____ (list a specific city or part of the country).
- ☐ I would like to work in another country _____ .
- ☐ I would like a job that might offer frequent transfers.
- ☐ I would like a job that will let me stay in one place.
- ☐ I would like a job that keeps me "on the road," traveling from place to place.
- ☐ I would like to work outdoors (list specifics if you can, i.e., in the woods, on a farm, at sea) _____ .
- ☐ I would like to work out of a car or truck most of the time.
- ☐ I would like to work in an office.
- ☐ I would like to work in my home.
- ☐ It's important to me that my work setting be pleasing to the eye.
- ☐ I would like to work in a garage or warehouse.
- ☐ I would like to work in a factory.
- ☐ I would like a job that involves both indoor and outdoor work.
- ☐ I would like to work in a science lab or hospital.
- ☐ I would like to work in a retail store.
- ☐ I would like to work in a restaurant.
- ☐ I would like to work on a constuction site.
- ☐ I would like to work on a ship, plane, train, or bus.
- ☐ I would like to work in a hotel or resort.
- ☐ I would like to work in a museum or art gallery.
- ☐ I would like to work in an art or photography studio.
- ☐ I would like to work in a concert hall or theater.
- ☐ I would like to work in a school or library.
- ☐ I would like to work in a church or synagogue.
- ☐ I would like to work on the set of a movie or TV show.
- ☐ I would like to work in a TV, radio or recording studio.
- ☐ I would like to work in _____ .

126

Working Conditions

Working conditions involve such things as what you like to work with and how you like to do your job. Consider your personality when you look at this list. Under what conditions do you feel most confident and at ease? What kinds of situations give you the most pleasure? How much structure do you like in your day? Do you like to be around people most of the time, or are you just as happy being alone? Do you like to meet new people, or are you more comfortable sticking with the same circle of friends and acquaintances? Check the statements below that appeal to you.

- ☐ I would like a job that requires me to "dress for success" (dress up for a professional office).
- ☐ I would like a job that requires me to wear a uniform or costume.
- ☐ I would like a job that lets me dress any way I want.
- ☐ I would like a job that lets me work alone most of the time.
- ☐ I would like a job that lets me work with the same group of people.
- ☐ I would like a job that lets me work with many different clients.
- ☐ I would like a job that lets me work with ideas.
- ☐ I would like a job that lets me work with information.
- ☐ I would like a job that lets me work with numbers.
- ☐ I would like a job that lets me work with machines.
- ☐ I would like a job that lets me work with tools.
- ☐ I would like a job that lets me be creative.
- ☐ I would like a job that involves physical labor or activity.
- ☐ I would like a job with prescribed duties and procedures.
- ☐ I would like a job with strict deadlines.
- ☐ I would like a job with structured working hours.
- ☐ I would like a job with somewhat flexible hours.
- ☐ I would like a job that lets me structure my time any way I want.
- ☐ I would like a job that often calls for putting in extra hours.
- ☐ I wouldn't mind working nights or weekends.
- ☐ I would like a job that involves risk or danger.
- ☐ I would like a job that might take away my privacy.
- ☐ I would like a job that is intellectually challenging.
- ☐ I would like a job I could forget about when I'm not there.
- ☐ I would like to be able to work part-time when my children are young.
- ☐ I would like a job that involves a variety of tasks and duties.
- ☐ Other _____

Relationships at Work

For many people, the social aspect of a job is one of its most important parts. A few years ago, there were predictions that a large number of people would soon be working at home, connected to their jobs by computer. It hasn't worked out that way. For most people, the rewards of working alone just don't make up for the isolation. For others, of course, they do. How much social contact do you expect from your job? Would you rather be the boss or the employee? Would you like to work with specific types of people? Check the statements below that appeal to you.

☐ I would like to work alone.
☐ I would like to work in a group or on a team.
☐ I would like to work with a variety of people.
☐ I would like to be the boss.
☐ I would like to be supervised by others.
☐ I would like to work for myself.
☐ I would like to work with adults.
☐ I would like to work with children.
☐ I would like to work with sick people.
☐ I would like to work with handicapped people.
☐ I would like to work with older people.
☐ I would like to work with creative people.
☐ I would like to work with people like me.
☐ I would like to work with people different from me.
☐ I would like to work with people who speak a different language.
☐ I would like to work with the underprivileged.
☐ I would like to teach people.
☐ I would like to entertain people.
☐ I would like to make people feel better.
☐ I would like to make people look better.
☐ I would like to help people get out of trouble.
☐ I would like to sell things to people.
☐ I would like to work with criminals.
☐ I would like to give people guidance.
☐ I would like to run for election to office.
☐ I would expect to socialize with my co-workers.
☐ I would like to meet celebrities on my job.
☐ I would like to work in a competitive environment.
☐ I would like a job where everyone works together for the common good.
☐ I would like to serve the public.
☐ I would like to serve private clients.
☐ Other _____

Psychological Rewards of Working

The psychological rewards of working relate to your passions and your values. For many people, these mean much more than financial gain. Can you imagine Mother Teresa giving up her work with the poor to become Donald Trump's administrative assistant? Did Martin Luther King, Jr., ever wish he'd gone into real estate sales? Did Chuck Yeager ever consider becoming an accountant? Would Whitney Houston enjoy a life as a computer programmer? Probably not. What do you expect to get from your job besides money? Check the statements below that appeal to you.

☐ I would like to be recognized in the community for the work I do.

☐ I would like a job where I am free to make my own decisions.

☐ I would like a job that furthers my mission in life.

☐ I would like a job that helps less fortunate members of the community.

☐ I would like a job that offer thrills and adventure.

☐ I would like a job that lets me put my family duties first.

☐ I would like a job in which I am continually learning something new.

☐ I would like a job that has high status in the community.

☐ I want to work with people I admire and respect.

☐ I would like a job that demands creativity and innovation.

☐ I would like to work for something I believe in, even if it is unpopular or puts me in danger.

☐ I would like a job that adds to the beauty in the world.

☐ I would like a job that adds to the safety of the world.

☐ I would like a position of power.

☐ I would like a job that gives me a lot of freedom.

☐ I want to feel secure that my job will be there as long as I want it.

☐ I would like to be applauded for my work.

☐ Other _____

Mixing Career and Family

While you are making career decisions, it is important to think about the kind of family life you want to have. Jobs that demand a great deal of travel or many evening and weekend hours in the office are usually not compatible with a close family life. On the other hand, if you want to have seven children, you need to think about careers that will financially support a family of that size. Today, both men and women have to be concerned about blending their career and family needs. Most women now work for pay, even when their children are very young. As a result, men need to be more involved with child care and household tasks. Since about half of all marriages end in divorce, also keep in mind that you cannot depend on the financial support of a spouse. Women, especially (90 percent of single parents are women), should prepare for careers with incomes that could support their families. Check the statements below that appeal to you.

- ☐ I want to be married.
- ☐ I want to have children.
- ☐ Family life is more important to me than my career.
- ☐ My career is more important to me than having a family.
- ☐ I would like both a rewarding career and a happy family life.
- ☐ I would like to stay home with my children when they are young.
- ☐ I would like my spouse to stay home with the children when they are young.
- ☐ I would like to work out of my house when my children are young.
- ☐ I would like a job with flexible hours so I can be available for my family.
- ☐ I would like to be able to afford to send my children to a day care pre-school.
- ☐ I would like to be able to afford to have a sitter come to the house.
- ☐ I would like to be able to afford to have live-in help with the children.
- ☐ I would like to be able to afford to have a housekeeper so I can spend more time with my family.
- ☐ I would expect my family to help out with household chores.
- ☐ Other _____

Financial Rewards

Financial rewards include not just *how much* money you make, but how you are paid, your benefits, job security, and so on. Check the statements below that appeal to you.

☐ I would like a job that pays at least $_____ per month. See page 91.

☐ I would like to be paid by the hour, with time and a half for overtime.

☐ I would like a monthly salary that doesn't vary with the number of hours I work.

☐ I would like to work on a commission basis.

☐ I would like a job that would be secure even in times of recession.

☐ I'm willing to accept a lower salary if the potential for either financial or psychological rewards is good.

☐ Money isn't important to me — I just need enough to get by.

☐ I want a job with good benefits (e.g., health insurance, pension plan, paid vacations).

☐ I'd like my salary to be based on my job performance.

☐ I'd like a job with scheduled pay increases.

☐ I'd like to be paid for the things I create or produce (e.g., paintings, articles, cookies).

☐ I'd like a job that offers bonuses or other incentives.

☐ I'm willing to start with a very low salary as long as there is an opportunity to work toward a very high salary.

☐ Other _____

Job Skills

This final category should help you fill out your general career outline. Check back to chapter two and record your findings below.

My physical skills include _____

_____

My intellectual and creative skills include _____

_____

My social skills include _____

_____

The skills I would like to acquire are (you will need to expand this list when you come up with a specific career goal)

_____

_____

_____

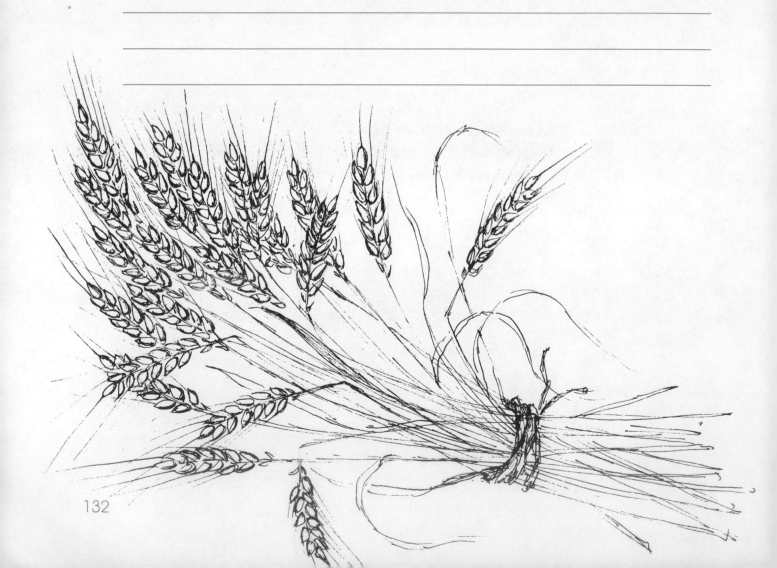

You probably checked a number of statements in each category. Read them all again to get a *very* broad picture of your career desires. Since it's unlikely that any job could meet all these requirements, go back and choose the one or two statements from each category that mean the most to you. Circle the boxes in front of those statements. Then enter them on the following chart. Keep these in mind as you begin shortening your list of possible careers.

Gena's chart looked like this:

The physical setting I want to work in is: <u>pleasing to the eye or an art museum or gallery</u>.

The working conditions I would most enjoy include: <u>a job that lets me work with many different clients and that lets me be creative</u>.

I would like my work relationships to be: <u>with creative people. I would also like to serve the public.</u>

The psychological reward most important to me is: <u>I must be continually learning something new</u>.

My goals for mixing career and family include: <u>having both a rewarding career and a happy family life, and being able to work out of my house while my children are young</u>.

Financially, I would like: <u>my salary based on my job performance</u>.

The skills I have or would most like to acquire include: <u>writing, doing research, and public speaking</u>.

133

Your Chart

The physical setting I want to work in is: _____

The working conditions I would most enjoy include: _____

_____

I would like my work relationships to be: _____

_____

The psychological reward most important to me is: _____

_____

My goals for mixing career and family include: _____

_____

Financially, I would like: _____

_____

The skills I have or would most like to acquire include: _____

_____

Do your answers support any of the career choices you had in mind? Do they rule out any of them? Or do they suggest new possibilities?

Gena found that her answers both narrowed and expanded her list of potential careers. She'd been thinking seriously about a career in business, possibly because both of her parents worked for large corporations. But that kind of job probably would not provide the kind of flexibility she'd like to have when her children are young. Besides, she wasn't sure she'd meet the most creative people working in business. Some of her answers, though, opened up new avenues of thought. She had always been interested in the arts. And her writing and researching skills could be used in a job that would let her keep on learning. Perhaps she could write about the arts or work in the public relations department of an art museum? With experience like that, she thought, she might be able to stay home and do free-lance writing projects during the time she was home with her children.

Consider Your Options

Another important point to remember is that workers today have many more options than they did 20 or 30 years ago. Technological advances have created hundreds of new jobs. Changes in society have brought about changes in the workplace: flexible hours, job sharing, and composite careers, for example, were unheard of in the not-too-distant past. And, more than ever before, people are going into business for themselves, creating their own careers and/or businesses.

Some people are enticed by these new possibilities. Others prefer to work in more traditional modes. The new ways of working will probably give you more freedom, but they usually also involve more risks and offer less security. They require a higher anxiety tolerance. Traditional jobs offer more security and are likely to be more comfortable for those with lower anxiety tolerance. Which category appeals to you? Before you choose, make sure you know what these terms mean. Here are some definitions.

Full-time job: A job calling for 35 to 40 hours or more of work each week.

Part-time job: A job at which you work less than 35 hours per week.

Structured hours: Strictly prescribed — and probably monitored — work hours. For example from 8:00 A.M. to 5:00 P.M., Monday through Friday. In some jobs, employers must insist that you be on the job at a particular time. For example, if you work in a store that opens at 9:00 A.M., your boss is not going to take your request to show up sometime between 9:00 and 10:30 very seriously. If you are the anchor for the 10:00 P.M. news, you had better be at your desk when the cameras start rolling.

Flexible hours: Work hours that provide more leeway. On some jobs, for example, you might be able to work any eight hours between 7:00 A.M. and 7:00 P.M. Many jobs offer a flexible starting time, but require all workers to be on the job during the busiest hours of the day. Self-employed people can be free to set their hours any way they like.

Composite careers: Having two or three jobs at the same time. For example, many college instructors are also researchers or writers. You might be a contractor and a cabinetmaker, or a lecturer and consultant. Many people combine more secure or higher paying jobs with higher risk or lower paying jobs. They probably get more satisfaction from the riskier career, but their other job provides more security. This is one way to "have your cake and eat it, too."

Working for salary: Being paid by the hour or the month.

Working on a free-lance or commission basis: Free-lancers are paid by the job. Salespeople and agents are paid commissions, usually a percentage of their sales. For example, if a real estate broker receives a commission of 6 percent, he or she would earn $6,000 for selling a $100,000 house.

Lifetime career: Having the same job, or same kind of job, throughout your working life.

Sequential careers: Having a series of different careers throughout your working life.

Anxiety: Worry or fear about future uncertainties. Anxiety isn't all bad, however. In fact, up to a certain point, it will help you do a better job. For example, if you are anxious about tomorrow's history test, you are more likely to prepare for it. And you may perform better than if you'd had no anxiety. (Why study if you're not worried?) If you are *too* anxious, however, your performance will suffer. You'll be too nervous to do a good job.

Anxiety tolerance: How well you can deal with fears and uncertainties. Some people like the feeling that "anything could happen," or are confident that they can deal with whatever problems come along. These people have high anxiety tolerance. Those with low anxiety tolerance find the worry and fear hard to deal with. It's hard to escape anxiety, however, so learning to tolerate the discomfort is important. Remember that these fears are normal. Everyone has them. Learning to act in spite of them is a mark of maturity.

On the chart below, circle the job characteristic on each line that appeals most to you.

Column 1	Column 2
Full-time	Part-time
Structured hours	Flexible hours
Employee	Employer
Salaried	Free-lance, commission
Single career	Composite careers
Lifetime career	Sequential careers

Did you circle more characteristics in column 1 or in column 2? _____

Column 1 represents careers with fewer risks, higher security, and less freedom. These careers also allow for a lower level of anxiety tolerance.

Column 2 represents careers with more risks, lower security, and more freedom. Careers like these usually call for a fairly high anxiety tolerance.

Do your choices feel right for you?	**Yes**	**No**	**Undecided**
Do you consider yourself a risk taker?	**Yes**	**No**	**Undecided**
Do you often worry about future events or situations?	**Yes**	**No**	**Undecided**

Refer to this chart as you make your career decisions and explore different job titles. Would you be more comfortable in a job offering security or one providing more freedom? Although these characteristics are at opposite ends of the scale, one is not better than the other. It's entirely a matter of what feels right for you.

137

Employee or Employer?

Another consideration, also based on your personality, is whether you would find it more rewarding to be an *employer* or an *employee*. Employers, as they relate to the following exercise, are defined as people who own their business, whatever its size. In other words, these people are *entrepreneurs*. They usually have more freedom and control over their time. However, they may often need to take major risks, both personal and financial. Is this an option that appeals to you?

ENTREPRENEURIAL CHECKLIST

Select the answer that best describes, or comes closest to, your feelings.

Willing to risk capital:

- ☐ 1. As long as I feel that there is a good chance of success, I'll go for it
- ☐ 2. I'm willing to invest some capital, but I always want to leave a sizable cushion, just in case.
- ☐ 3. I have never really felt comfortable risking money or time on things I'm not absolutely sure of.

Independence:

- ☐ 1. Most of all, I want to be my own boss; it's my major goal.
- ☐ 2. I don't mind working for other people, but I'd rather be on my own.
- ☐ 3. Being on my own really scares me. I'd rather have the security of being an employee, and let someone else worry about the problems.

Flexibility:

- ☐ 1. I adapt to change quickly and decisively.
- ☐ 2. I move, but it takes time and careful consideration.
- ☐ 3. I would rather see things stay the same; I get uptight when change occurs.

Self-confidence:

- ☐ 1. I am very confident in myself and know that I can handle most situations.
- ☐ 2. I am confident most of the time, particularly when I know the ground rules.
- ☐ 3. I'm not in control of my destiny; other people really control my future.

Attitude toward people:

- ☐ 1. I am naturally drawn to people; I like them, and they like me.
- ☐ 2. I find most people enjoyable, and most people are attracted to me.
- ☐ 3. I like things more than people and don't have many friends.

Knowledge of the particular business:

- ☐ 1. I know the business that I've been thinking about well and will enjoy it.
- ☐ 2. I'm reasonably confident I can learn the business, and it appears that I will enjoy it.
- ☐ 3. I am not familiar with this type of business, nor do I know whether I will enjoy it.

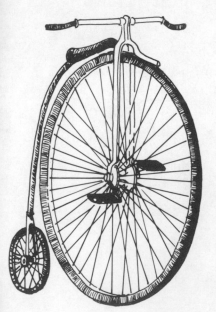

Ability to start from scratch:

☐ 1. I enjoy the challenge of building something from scratch on my own; I'm a self-starter.

☐ 2. If given basic guidelines, I can do a good job.

☐ 3. I really prefer to have the entire job laid out, then I'll do it well.

Commitment:

☐ 1. I have a high drive and commitment, and won't stop until the project is done.

☐ 2. I seem to have a higher level of perseverance when things are going well.

☐ 3. I start many projects, but rarely find time to finish them.

Common sense:

☐ 1. I consider myself realistic and "street wise" when it comes to business.

☐ 2. Most business situations make sense, but there are areas where I feel out of step.

☐ 3. I am inexperienced and impractical in business matters.

Willingness to accept failure:

☐ 1. "Nothing ventured, nothing gained" is my motto.

☐ 2. I want to succeed, but if I fail, I will accept it.

☐ 3. I want to avoid failure, and won't take a risk if it doesn't look like a sure thing.

Health:

☐ 1. I have excellent health and feel good, both physically and mentally.

☐ 2. I get sick on occasion, but it doesn't last long.

☐ 3. I have problems with my health, illness always seems to get in my way.

Work habits:

☐ 1. I plan before I start and then work my plan; I'm well-organized.

☐ 2. I find that I'm organized most of the time; but on occasion, I do get out of control.

☐ 3. I take things as they come, and sometimes get priorities confused.

To total your score, add up all the checked numbers. A number one has the weight of one, a number two scores a two and a three equals three. If your total score is between 12 and 16, you are a good candidate and should consider starting your own business at some time.

This checklist is for self-evaluation of your personal characteristics, to see if you will have a better-than-average chance of success as an entrepreneur. The material may touch on some tender personal areas; you'll have to be honest with yourself. Be careful to avoid self-deception; don't brush the negative under the rug.

Take enough time to evaluate the criteria and information, and try to relate some actual experiences from your past. Determine how you will handle things when it gets tough. Because, if you can count on anything, you can count on the fact that owning your own business operation is going to be tough.

This short personal appraisal is by no means an evaluation of whether you are qualified to be an entrepreneur. It is simply a way of focusing on your personal attributes, and it may help you decide on taking that major step. You may want to ask a few of your close friends or relatives to evaluate you, perhaps more objectively than you can do it yourself.

Reprinted with permission: *How To Start, Expand and Sell A Business, A Complete Guidebook for Entrepreneurs* by James C. Comiskey.

What About Status?

As a teen in America today, you are probably well acquainted with the concept of status. It usually comes attached to a brand name, though those names may vary widely from place to place. It's expensive. And it's more important to some people than it is to others.

Basically, the same rules apply to the perceived status of different careers. Certain job titles, like certain brands of jeans, offer more prestige. What is considered a high-status job may vary in different groups or circles, however. For example, a philosopher might have high status in intellectual circles, but hardly any among business-oriented groups.

Sometimes higher status is assigned to people in professions that require more education: doctors, lawyers, college professors, and so on. Sometimes it relates to the respect society bestows on groups like the clergy. The arts, too, seem to have a certain prestige. A few jobs — in the military or the diplomatic corps, for example — come with assigned ranks so there can be no mistakes about status. In fields like sales, prestige is related to what you sell. Someone in estate jewelry, for example, will have higher status than someone who sells parts from junked cars.

Interestingly, though, status does not necessarily relate to income. That junk dealer could earn much more than the jewelry salesperson — or the doctor, for that matter. Some jobs that require just a year or two of vocational training offer higher pay than many careers calling for a college degree. Plumbers and electricians, for example, have a higher average salary than teachers and librarians. In other words, like the "right" kind of shoes, status can be expensive.

That's why you need to give some thought to your own values as you consider your job choices. In itself, status is neither good nor bad. Because some people place so much importance on it, however, it is easy to confuse your own feelings with those of your friends or parents. During your teen years, especially, peer pressure is strong. It also usually attaches the most status to meeting sex-role stereotypes: men should be strong and brave, women should be pretty and not too bright. Should you make choices for your future based on these pressures? No. Remember that they will begin decreasing shortly. It will become easier to be your own person. Remember, too, that your friends will not be working at your chosen career. You will.

What does status mean to you? Whose opinions matter to you most? What values does status reflect? Can you explain why, today, a rock star has more status than a teacher or a politician? Consider these questions and then, to help clarify your thoughts, indicate whether you agree or disagree with the following statements.

It is important to me to have a job with high status.

Agree   Disagree

I am willing to invest the time it takes to train for a job with high status.

Agree   Disagree

It is more important to me that a job has status than that it pays well.

Agree   Disagree

I don't think I could be happy at a job that others might look down on.

Agree   Disagree

141

CHAPTER SIX

Career Research

Reading about careers isn't enough

Choose a job you love, and you will never
have to work a day in your life.
—Confucius

Every calling is great when greatly pursued.
—Oliver Wendell Holmes, Jr.

Section Two:
WHAT DO I WANT?

Marta had a dream. She didn't know exactly where she was, but it was warm and faraway. And it was beautiful. Lots of people were around, but everyone seemed to be doing his or her own thing. They were all wearing shorts and T-shirts, and they worked diligently with what appeared to be tiny tools or instruments. Periodically, someone would shout excitedly, and everyone else would cheer. This went on until a brilliant sunset brought on the night. Marta woke up feeling content, but puzzled. When she shared her dream with her friend, Jennifer, she said, "I wonder what it was all about. I'd like to go back there, wherever it was."

"Sounds like some kind of archaeological dig to me," Jennifer replied.

"What's that?"

"You know. It's like looking for bones or tools or any kind of remnant of past civilizations. Archaeologists go out and recover these things, and then they study them and help put together a picture of what life was like at a certain time and place."

"Oh, yeah? That sounds like something I might like to do."

Now that you've considered some of the general characteristics you'd like in a job, it's time to get more specific. As you work through this chapter, you will identify several jobs that might meet your requirements and then set out to learn as much about them as you can.

Perhaps you've already thought of some careers you'd like to know more about. If not, now's the time to start. Can you, like Marta, picture an ideal job? In addition to the work itself, think about the settings and the situations it might involve. Would you find them pleasing day-in and day-out, year after year? Take some time to daydream about your future career. Shut your eyes for a few minutes and consider different possibilities. Wait until one feels right and you, too, feel content.

In order to select a career you'll be happy with, you should have some knowledge of the many jobs available. There are thousands of them, and we can't list them all here. But the *Guide for Occupational Exploration (GOE)* makes things a little easier by organizing them into 12 interest groups and 66 worker trait groups.

The jobs in each category have certain things in common. Therefore, by investigating the groups that appeal most to you, you may come up with a number of possible careers. We've listed the interest groups below, along with a few jobs in each category. For a much longer list, go to your school or public library.

The interest groups are as follows:

Artistic: People in this group are interested in the creative expression of feelings or ideas. Possible careers include creative writing, editing, studio art, commercial art, acting, directing, modeling, singing, playing an instrument, composing, and arts and crafts.

Protective: Workers in this category are interested in using authority to protect people and property. Careers include police officers, investigators, security guards, fire fighters, ambulance drivers, prison guards, wardens, probation officers, body guards, and law enforcement officials.

Scientific: An interest in discovering, collecting, and analyzing information about the natural world and in applying scientific research findings to problems in medicine, life sciences, and natural science is essential here. Careers include theoretical research, medicine and surgery, dentistry, veterinary medicine, and laboratory technicians of all kinds.

Mechanical: If you are interested in applying mechanical principles to practical situations, using machines, handtools, or techniques, you might find careers in this category satisfying. They include mechanical engineering, maintenance and construction, surveying, drafting, environmental protection, plumbing and pipefitting, electrical work, drilling and oil exploration, welding, and truck driving.

Plants and animals: To be happy working at the jobs in this category, you should have an interest in activities involving plants and animals, usually in an outdoor setting. Possible careers include farming, forestry, nursery and groundskeeping, animal training or services, floristry, landscape architecture, or owning or operating agricultural businesses or services.

Industrial: Workers in this category should have an interest in repetitive, concrete, organized activities in a factory setting. Jobs include factory supervision and instruction, machine setup and operation, precision handwork, inspection, machine operation, manual assembly, casting and molding, laundering, dry cleaning, wrapping and packing, cleaning, hoisting, and conveying.

Business detail: These jobs require an interest in organized, clearly defined activities requiring accuracy and attention to detail, primarily in an office setting. Careers include office administration, secretarial work, bookkeeping and auditing, accounting, statistical reporting and analysis, computer operation, reception, and information giving.

Selling: Workers in this category have an interest in bringing others to a point of view through personal persuasion, using sales and promotion techniques. Careers include wholesale and retail sales, real estate sales, sales demonstration, technical sales, and sales promotion.

Accommodating: An interest in catering to the wishes of others, usually on a one-to-one basis is required for job satisfaction here. Careers include tour guide or travel services, food services, cosmetology, physical conditioning, driving taxis or buses, chauffeuring, doorkeeping, and ticket taking.

Humanitarian: These workers have an interest in helping others with their mental, spiritual, social, physical, or vocational needs. Careers include counseling, social work, nursing, therapy and rehabilitation, specialized teaching, and religious occupations.

Leading-influencing: An interest in leading and influencing others through activities involving high-level verbal or numerical skills is important in these careers. They include teaching, data analysis, library services, justice administration, legal practice, government administration, translating and interpreting, fund raising and public relations, business management, and budget and financial control.

Physical performing: This category calls for an interest in physical activities performed before an audience. Professional athletes, coaches and instructors, and officiators fall into this category, as do such performers as jugglers, acrobats, and high wire walkers.

The GOE's system is just one way of classifying different types of jobs. As you look through your library's career research section, you will find others. There may be books about careers in finance, high-tech careers, jobs of the future, careers in the arts, and so on. Which two categories sound most interesting to you? Write them below and then check the library for particular jobs within each interest area. This is where your career research begins.

Bring In Your Identity

The career interest areas are set up so that the jobs listed in each category reflect similar values. Turn back to your Bull's Eye Chart on page 27 to review your values and passions (passions also reflect your values). Now go over the interest areas again. Below, list one or two that appeal to you most, or that seem to complement your values and passions.

_____

_____

While you're at it, take another look at your strengths and skills. Do you see (or can you think of) any careers within your chosen interest area(s) that also seem to fit in with these aspects of your personality? List some possible careers on the following lines. (Don't forget to consult your chart from chapter 5!)

_____

_____

_____

When Letitia looked back at her chart, she saw that her highest values were power, helping others, and personal integrity and moral courage. Looking again at her list of passions, politics and social justice seemed to be the ones that she most wanted to be a part of her career. As she looked again at the career interest areas, she decided the humanitarian and leading-influencing categories were most appropriate for her.

Letitia scored high in both the dominating and influencing areas on her personal strengths test. Writing, researching, and persuading are among her skills. Therefore, she decided that becoming a lawyer was a wise choice for her. Two other careers she hadn't thought about also looked appealing — counseling and government administration. Letitia added them to her list of jobs to do more research on.

Career Research

An old proverb says, "Tell me and I forget. Show me and I remember. But involve me and I understand." Your career research will involve all three of these steps.

Career research begins with traditional library investigation. This is an essential part of your project. Many people make a career choice after completing this step, but stopping your research at this point is a little like marrying someone you've heard about, but have only just met. The information you gather will not be truly meaningful until you combine it with observation and experience.

Choosing a career (like choosing a marriage partner) is one of the most important decisions you will ever make. So take the time and energy necessary to do the job right. Complete all three steps in the process.

Remember that the choices you are making now are *tentative*. You may change your mind many times before settling on your future course. In this chapter, you will make a career decision. But it is meant to be used for the rest of the *book*, not necessarily for the rest of your life. The *process* you are learning, however, *can* be useful over a lifetime, no matter how many career changes you make.

STEP ONE

Does your school have a computerized career information system? If so, this is an excellent way to begin your research.

If not, start your research at your school or public library. Does it have a Career Information Center? If so, most of the information you will need can be located there. If not, look under the heading *careers* in the card catalog, microfilm reader, or data bank to locate all available books on the subject. Check, too, under the career areas you find most interesting (agriculture, business, science, and so on).

Most libraries will have three important reference books, all published by the U.S. Department of Labor. They are the *Dictionary of Occupational Titles (DOT)*, the *Occupational Outlook Handbook (OOH)*, and the source you are now acquainted with, the *Guide for Occupational Exploration*.

Going to the GOE itself will give you additional information on its interest groups and worker trait groups, as well as listings of jobs within each category. It will tell you about the work and about the skills, abilities, interests, and aptitudes of those who do it. Information on the education or training required to get a job in a particular field is also included.

You will find job descriptions for more than 20,000 careers in the DOT. Don't be put off by the book's size. It's really very easy to use. Turn to the alphabetical index of occupational titles and locate the title of the job you are investigating. You will find a nine-digit code number next to the job title. Then simply turn to that number in the front section of the book. There you will find your job description.

Keep a record of the DOT numbers for careers that interest you. Many other references also use these numbers to organize career data.

The OOH is another valuable source. It's updated every two years, so be sure to get the most recent edition. It will give you up-to-date information on over two hundred careers including such things as required education or training, typical working hours, working conditions, expected earnings, the outlook for this job, and sources of additional information.

You might also want to check the *Occupational Outlook Quarterly*, a supplement published four times a year with news of trends in the job market.

Magazines are also good sources of career information. Because most of them are published every week or every month, they are often the first to note the latest trends or developments. Articles about your field of interest will be indexed in the *Reader's Guide to Periodical Literature*. Subjects are arranged alphabetically. Any articles on your topic that have been published during the time period covered by the *Guide* will be listed under your subject. Listings include the name and date of the publication, the title of the article, and the pages on which it is located. Articles may become quickly outdated, so don't bother looking for information that was published much more than a year or two ago.

Ask your librarian what other materials are available. Sometimes pamphlets and special reports about specific careers are kept in file cabinets. Your library might also have videotapes, filmstrips, or other audiovisual materials on careers.

It's also helpful to read your local want ads. Make this a habit. They will give you a feeling for the number and kinds of jobs currently available in your area.

CARL'S STORY

Carl spent a great deal of time thinking about what he wanted to do, but he was still uncertain. One day he went to a library and began reading his way to his future. He went from section to section — travel, psychology, architecture — paging through books to see how he felt, what held his interest, what he wanted to know more about. When he reached the business section, he started to feel at home. He was fascinated by everything he read and wanted to know much more. Based on this excursion, Carl investigated business careers more seriously. His interest held. Today, he is a successful and satisfied owner of a securities brokerage house.

Career Interest Survey

Now it's time to choose three careers that appeal to you most and begin learning as much about them as you can. Review the careers chosen on page 147. It will be helpful if you can interview people now working in these fields as well. Separate worksheets are provided for each job.

JOB TITLE _____

1. What specific tasks would I perform on this job? (For example, a salesclerk would answer questions, tidy displays, unpack merchandise, write sales slips, make change, and so on.)

_____

_____

2. What is the job environment likely to be? Is this compatible with the setting I said I wanted on *page 126*?

_____

_____

3. What would be the rewards of working at this job? Are they the same as the ones I listed on *page 129*?

_____

_____

4. I would find this job particularly satisfying because: (Review your passions, values, interests, and life goals for guidance). *See page 27.*

_____

_____

5. Is this job compatible with my work behavioral style? If so, in what ways? (Don't feel obliged to answer this question unless you have been able to take the complete Personal Profile System.)

_____

_____

6. How much training or education would I need? Where could I get it? Am I willing to make this kind of commitment? *Review pages 116 – 120.*

_____

_____

7. Does this job require specific physical attributes or abilities (strength or health requirements, 20/20 vision, and so on)? If so, what are they? Do I meet them?

_____

_____

8. What could I expect to earn as a beginner in this field? _____

What is the average mid-career salary? _____

9. Does this meet my salary requirements? *See pages 92 and 131.*   Yes   No

_____

10. What is the projected outlook for this career? Will there be many job openings when I am ready to go to work?

_____

_____

11. What aptitudes, strengths, and talents does this job call for? Do I have them? Can I get them? *See page 132.*

_____

_____

12. What can I do today to begin preparing for this job?

_____

_____

13. What classes must I take in high school to qualify for this job?

_____

_____

14. Where in this town or state could I find a job in this field?

_____

15. How does this career mesh with my family plans? Is it consistent with my desired lifestyle? *See page 130.* Does it offer opportunities for flexible hours or part-time work? Is the income high enough so I could maintain my family on it alone if necessary? Could I afford the kind of day care I'd like for my children?

_____

_____

_____

16. Are there opportunities for self-employment in this field (free-lance work, consulting, and the like)?

_____

_____

JOB TITLE _____

1. What specific tasks would I perform on this job? (For example, a salesclerk would answer questions, tidy displays, unpack merchandise, write sales slips, make change, and so on.)

_____

_____

2. What is the job environment likely to be? Is this compatible with the setting I said I wanted on *page 126*?

_____

_____

3. What would be the rewards of working at this job? Are they the same as the ones I listed on *page 129*?

_____

_____

4. I would find this job particularly satisfying because: (Review your passions, values, interests, and life goals for guidance). *See page 27.*

_____

_____

5. Is this job compatible with my work behavioral style? If so, in what ways? (Don't feel obliged to answer this question unless you have been able to take the complete Personal Profile System.)

_____

_____

6. How much training or education would I need? Where could I get it? Am I willing to make this kind of commitment? *Review pages 116 – 120.*

_____

_____

7. Does this job require specific physical attributes or abilities (strength or health requirements, 20/20 vision, and so on)? If so, what are they? Do I meet them?

_____

_____

8. What could I expect to earn as a beginner in this field? _____

What is the average mid-career salary? _____

9. Does this meet my salary requirements? *See pages 92 and 131.*   Yes   No

_____

10. What is the projected outlook for this career? Will there be many job openings when I am ready to go to work?

_____

_____

11. What aptitudes, strengths, and talents does this job call for? Do I have them? Can I get them? *See page 132.*

_____

_____

12. What can I do today to begin preparing for this job?

_____

_____

13. What classes must I take in high school to qualify for this job?

_____

_____

14. Where in this town or state could I find a job in this field?

_____

15. How does this career mesh with my family plans? Is it consistent with my desired lifestyle? *See page 130.* Does it offer opportunities for flexible hours or part-time work? Is the income high enough so I could maintain my family on it alone if necessary? Could I afford the kind of day care I'd like for my children?

_____

_____

16. Are there opportunities for self-employment in this field (free-lance work, consulting, and the like)?

_____

_____

JOB TITLE _____

1. What specific tasks would I perform on this job? (For example, a salesclerk would answer questions, tidy displays, unpack merchandise, write sales slips, make change, and so on.)

_____

_____

2. What is the job environment likely to be? Is this compatible with the setting I said I wanted on *page 126*?

_____

_____

3. What would be the rewards of working at this job? Are they the same as the ones I listed on *page 129*?

_____

_____

4. I would find this job particularly satisfying because (Review your passions, values, interests, and life goals for guidance). *See page 27.*

_____

_____

5. Is this job compatible with my work behavioral style? If so, in what ways? (Don't feel obliged to answer this question unless you have been able to take the complete Personal Profile System.)

_____

_____

6. How much training or education would I need? Where could I get it? Am I willing to make this kind of commitment? *Review pages 116 – 120.*

_____

_____

7. Does this job require specific physical attributes or abilities (strength or health requirements, 20/20 vision, and so on)? If so, what are they? Do I meet them?

_____

_____

8. What could I expect to earn as a beginner in this field? _____

What is the average mid-career salary? _____

9. Does this meet my salary requirements? *See pages 92 and 131.*　　　Yes　　　No

_____

10. What is the projected outlook for this career? Will there be many job openings when I am ready to go to work?

_____

_____

11. What aptitudes, strengths, and talents does this job call for? Do I have them? Can I get them? *See page 132.*

_____

_____

12. What can I do today to begin preparing for this job?

_____

_____

13. What classes must I take in high school to qualify for this job?

_____

_____

14. Where in this town or state could I find a job in this field?

_____

_____

15. How does this career mesh with my family plans? Is it consistent with my desired lifestyle? *See page 130.* Does it offer opportunities for flexible hours or part-time work? Is the income high enough so I could maintain my family on it alone if necessary? Could I afford the kind of day care I'd like for my children?

_____

_____

_____

16. Are there opportunities for self-employment in this field (free-lance work, consulting, and the like)?

_____

_____

155

STEP TWO

SHOW ME AND I REMEMBER

The popularity of how-to videos is evidence that this statement is true. Books about working out or cooking or playing tennis are often cheaper and provide more information than videos do. But somehow seeing Jimmy Connors hit a perfect serve or Jane Fonda "go for the burn" makes a more lasting impression.

As you completed your three job surveys, one of your choices probably emerged as the favorite. If two or more of the jobs still hold strong appeal for you, choose the one you are least familiar with for this part of your research. If you discovered that none of the careers you investigated meets your requirements, make some new choices and go through the research and survey process once more. Again, remember that this is a tentative decision, a trial choice. Don't feel you are obligated to stick with this career simply because you are choosing it now.

When you have completed your survey and interviewed someone now working in the field of your choice, you are ready to begin step two.

VISUALIZATION

Picture yourself on the job. What would a typical working day be like? Use the information you gathered in step one to answer the following questions. Sit down, close your eyes, and actually *see* yourself going through the day. Pay particular attention to your feelings. Concern yourself with more than just the work. How would you feel in the morning as you got ready to leave home? What would you do at lunch? How would you feel at the end of the day? How would you spend your evening?

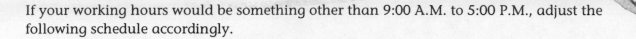

If your working hours would be something other than 9:00 A.M. to 5:00 P.M., adjust the following schedule accordingly.

7:00 A.M. Getting ready for work. What would you wear? How do you feel about going to work? Are you looking forward to the day? _____

_____

8:00 A.M. Traveling to work. How would you get there? How far would you travel? Or would you work at home? _____

_____

9:00 A.M. Walking into work. Describe the setting. Who else is there? What kind of greeting do you get from them? _____

_____

9:00 A.M. to 12:00 noon. What would you be doing during this time? If this is a typical day, what tasks and responsibilities would you carry out?

_____

10:00 A.M. _____

11:00 A.M. _____

Noon. Where would you have lunch, and with whom? Would you socialize with co-workers? Clients?

_____

_____

1:00 P.M. to 5:00 P.M. As the day goes on, see yourself handling some special problems or challenges that might arise in this field. What are they? How do you deal with them? _____

_____

1:00 P.M. _____

2:00 P.M. _____

3:00 P.M. _____

4:00 P.M. _____

5:00 P.M. _____

6:00 P.M. Going home. How do you feel at the end of the day? What might you be thinking about? _____

_____

7:00 P.M. and on. How would you spend a typical evening? Would you need to bring work home? Would you be with your family? Your friends? Are there hobbies or volunteer activities you would want to pursue?

_____

_____

157

The Shadow Program

How difficult was it for you to see yourself on the job? Chances are, despite all your research, some of the questions were hard to answer. This exercise is meant to help you get the kind of information not likely to be found in books.

The shadow program actually lets you spend a day watching someone perform the job you want to have. First, of course, you have to get that person's permission. Write a business letter to the person of your choice, explaining what you want to do: You want to follow this person around for a day. You want to stand in the back of the room. You *do not* want to get in the way. You *do not* expect this person to spend much time with you or answer your questions during work hours. You *would*, however, like to have some time at lunch or after work to ask questions about the things you've seen. (Be sure to bring a notebook and pen so you can record your impressions and jot down any questions that occur to you during the day.)

Your letter should be neatly typed (or, if you use a computer, printed out on a letter-quality printer). Keep it short and to the point, but be sure to state why it is important to you to observe someone doing this job. State that you will call on a given day to get the person's response and set up an appointment if he or she is willing to take part in this program. And be sure to say thank you.

> Important note: Don't forget to send a handwritten thank you note soon after your day as a shadow.

Your letter might look something like the one below.

1426 Washington Street
Kansas City, MO 64113
April 6, 1991

Ms. Roberta Ekholm
ABC Advertising
1100 Walnut Drive
Kansas City, MO 64104

Dear Ms. Ekholm:

I am a student at Braddock School and, I hope, a future advertising copywriter. Would you be willing to let me spend a day as your "shadow" so I can learn more about what this work entails?

As your shadow, I would remain quietly in the background as you go about your daily tasks. I know that you are a busy person, and I would not expect you to take time out from your usual schedule. I would, however, appreciate it if you could take half an hour to answer my questions at the end of the day.

Although I've done thorough research on copywriting, I feel a day on the job — even in the background — would tell me so much more than I can learn from books. I will call you on Monday, April 15, to get your response. If you are willing to help me, perhaps we can schedule a day that would be convenient for you to have me around.

Thank you for your time and consideration.

Yours truly,

Don Garibaldi

Don Garibaldi
456-6789

STEP THREE

INVOLVE ME AND I UNDERSTAND

One of the best ways to decide whether your career choice is a good one is to get a job in that field. You won't actually be working at your dream job, of course. But, by putting yourself in a position to watch other people do that kind of work, you can get an accurate picture of what it's like.

Your goal, then, is to get an entry-level job that puts you in contact with people in your chosen career. Not all jobs in your chosen field will do that. For example, delivering newspapers won't tell you very much about what it's like to be a reporter, but answering phones at the newspaper office might be enlightening.

It's fairly easy to come up with entry-level jobs for some careers. Future doctors or nurses, for example, can be candy stripers at the local hospital. Future cooks or restaurateurs might be able to bus dishes at the best restaurant in town.

But what if you want to be a buyer for a department store? Or a lawyer? If a job doesn't come immediately to mind, take some time to think things through. Where do the people in your career field work? An office? A courthouse? A garage? What other kinds of jobs do people do in these settings? Can you do any of those jobs?

Practice your skill at recognizing entry-level jobs by thinking of possible positions for people interested in the following careers. In column A list paying jobs that will expose you to the work of each career.

Example: Mechanic = gas jockey, auto parts sales, or cashier

CAREER	COLUMN A PAID	COLUMN B VOLUNTEER
Attorney		
Social worker		
Accountant		
Veterinarian		
Police officer		
Retail salesperson		
Classical musician		
Politician		
Hairstylist		
Office manager		

(Hint: If all else fails, most businesses will allow you to come in for a few hours each week and run errands.)

Keep the following points in mind as you go about your entry-level job:

1. It may not be fun or interesting. Although it's hard to stick with a job that's boring — or even nasty — keep your goal in mind. Remember that you won't have to do this forever.

2. It may not pay well; it may not pay at all. The point of this job is to learn, not necessarily to earn. If you need to volunteer your services in order to get where you want to be, do so. Many charities and social service agencies in your community will have volunteer opportunities relating to specific career fields. For example, if you're interested in a law career, you may be able to volunteer for the legal aid society. In column B on the preceding page, list volunteer jobs you could do that would put you in contact with an interesting career possibility.

Once you have a job in your chosen area of interest, observe what is going on around you. Pay attention to your feelings. Do you like the setting? Do you feel comfortable? Does what is happening get you excited? Does the pace of the day match your personality? Is the level of responsibility comfortable or threatening? Does the work hold your interest, or could this be boring after a short time? Do you like the people you work with? How do they seem to feel about their jobs? Are they bored? Challenged? Overworked? About how many hours a week do they work? Do they take work home with them? Are they expected to take part in after-work activities (sports, entertaining clients, and the like)? Do they travel? How often and for how long?

Your answers to questions like these should tell you whether to go ahead with your career plans or if you need to make new ones. Answer them honestly, and don't feel bad if you decide to make a change. It's much easier to do so now than it will be after you've invested years in training.

The Chemistry Test

When the senior class at Nicholson Hall decided to hold a dance to raise money for the homeless, class officers Jacob, Coretta, George, and Joan drew lots to decide who would be in charge of what. As a result, Coretta was designated to make centerpieces, George became the treasurer, Jacob was delegated to selling tickets, and Joan was chair of the entire event.

Things did not go well. Jacob sent the tickets back three times before they were printed to his satisfaction. And the thought of asking people he didn't know well to buy them made him feel quite ill at ease.

Joan needed to be sure that everyone was in agreement before she made any decisions. As a result, meetings went on for hours and everyone was frustrated.

Coretta preferred to take her own course rather than follow the directions on assembling the centerpieces. Details like that just didn't interest her. None of the decorations came out looking the same, though Coretta tried to tell everyone that they were more interesting this way.

George was into creative bookkeeping. He didn't like solitary activities like this, but when he tried to keep the books while carrying on a conversation with a friend, he made a number of mistakes.

With everything in chaos, the group was about ready to cancel the dance altogether. Then they remembered what they had learned about work behavior styles and their own personal styles in class. Assessing their strengths, they found that each had a preferred behavior style:

Coretta — dominance

George — influencing

Joan — steadiness

Jacob — compliance

They reassigned the duties, this time choosing the person who was best suited to each job. Since Coretta liked to be in charge and make decisions, she became the chair. George, the influencer, was a natural to take over ticket sales. Joan liked working with explicit instructions so she loved being in charge of the decorations. And Jacob, as treasurer, made sure every cent was accounted for. Accuracy was extremely important to him.

As the dance committee's story shows, your work behavior style affects the way you perform — *and the way you feel about* — a job. Turn back to page 43 and review the four classic work styles. Everyone has to be able to use each of the styles to some extent, but one of them is probably the most comfortable for you. Which one?

Match the four people described below with the career that would pass his or her chemistry test in each of the work settings listed. If you were in charge of these businesses, which employee would you put in which job?

Ellen's preferred behavior style is dominance. She is a high-energy individual who likes to be in charge of what she is doing. She is decisive and always looks for the most efficient way to do things. She likes to solve problems, is comfortable with change, and is very goal directed.

Robert's style is influencing. He is a creative person who likes flexibility in his work environment. He is gregarious and likes to work with people. Robert's enthusiasm can be contagious. He is good at persuading people to act. He likes varied tasks and will take calculated risks.

Michiko is most comfortable with steadiness. She likes to work with other people, particularly in a supportive role. A patient and considerate person, Michiko likes tasks with well-defined procedures. A steady worker, she follows her projects through from beginning to end. She is a listener and a doer.

Romero's preferred style is compliance. He is extremely detail oriented and is likely to question the decisions of others. He wants to know the facts behind the issues. A conscientious worker, he is precise in any task he undertakes and wants to make sure it is done accurately.

How would you assign the following jobs to these four individuals?

Example: In a book publishing company, jobs would be assigned as follows:

BOOK PUBLISHING

Publisher: *Ellen*

Sales rep: *Robert*

Book designer: *Michiko*

Editor: *Romero*

CONSTRUCTION

Draftsperon _____

Contractor _____

Architect _____

Carpenter _____

FACTORY

Cafeteria chef _____

Assembly line worker _____

Foreman _____

Quality control inspector _____

BANK

Loan officer _____

Bank teller _____

Manager _____

Accountant _____

HOSPITAL

Minister/priest/rabbi _____

Administrator _____

Lab technician _____

Physician _____

SCHOOL

Secretary _____

Principal _____

Attendance clerk _____

Counselor _____

RESEARCH LAB

Project manager _____

Fund raiser _____

Scientist _____

Computer programmer _____

Even within career categories, certain specialties may be more suited to one behavior style than to the others. Can you identify which personality type would likely be happiest in each of the jobs below? Review the definitions of behavioral styles on page 43. Then assign a style to each of these jobs. Each grouping contains one of each of the four styles. Although this is not an exact science, see what makes sense to you. Be prepared to defend you choices in discussion.

WRITER

Freelance magazine writer: *dominance*
Copywriter for advertising agency: *influencing*
Reporter for local newspaper: *steadiness*
Technical writer for science textbooks: *compliance*

PHYSICIAN

Anesthesiologist _____

Surgeon _____

Chief of physicians at local hospital _____

Teacher at medical school _____

TEACHER

Teacher in public school system _____

Private tutor or coach _____

Professor of accounting at university level _____

Trainer for major corporation _____

CHEF

Head chef in a large restaurant — tastes everything! _____

Catering company owner _____

Teacher of adult education cooking classes _____

Associate chef in a restaurant _____

164

Answers:

Dominance: Freelance magazine writer, chief of physicians, private tutor or coach, catering company owner

   People in these jobs are all self-directed. They are in charge.

Influencing: Copywriter, teacher at medical school, trainer for major corporation, teacher of adult education cooking classes

   People in these careers work closely with others and are involved with teaching or influencing them.

Steadiness: Reporter for local newspaper, anesthesiologist, teacher in public school system, associate chef in restaurant

   These workers like a highly defined set of procedures. They enjoy supportive, predictable roles.

Compliance: Technical writer for science textbooks, surgeon, professor of accounting at university level, head chef in large restaurant

   People in these jobs are precise and exacting and concerned about quality control.

Which career seems to be your favorite choice at this point in time?. What work behavior style do you think would be prominent in someone happy with this job?

_____

Why? _____

_____

Does this match your personal work style? Review your answers on page 42.

                    Yes   No   Perhaps

In what ways? _____

_____

To gain a better understanding of your own style, ask your teacher or counselor for information about taking a Personal Profile System test. Or see page 288 on how to get a copy. It will help you clarify this important issue.

Has your research led you to a tentative career choice? If not, the next chapter offers a model you can use to help make this — or any — decision.

Adapted with permission from the *Personal Profile System*, Carlson Learning Company, MN.

No trumpets sound when the important
decisions of our life are made. Destiny is
made known silently.
                              —Agnes De Mille

Choice, not chance, determines destiny.
                              —Anonymous

CHAPTER SEVEN

Decision Making

How to choose what's best for you

Section Two:
WHAT DO I WANT?

Quint was starting his junior year of high school, and, as his parents never seemed to tire of telling him, it was time to make some decisions about his future. Quint wondered why he should bother. Everyone else seemed to know exactly what he should do.

His parents wanted Quint to attend their alma mater, a private college in another state. His football coach said that, if he attended the local junior college, Quint was sure to be a starter on the team there. And, if he did well, he might even be able to play for a four-year school after that. Ms. Watson, his math teacher, thought Quint should attend the state university, which had an excellent engineering program. His friends wanted Quint to join them on a cross-country motorcycle trip. They all needed a break from school, they said.

But what did he want? Quint wasn't sure, and he didn't really like to think about it. He wished the whole subject would just go away.

Making decisions can be difficult for a young adult. You grow up learning to please your parents or your teachers. Then, suddenly, you're supposed to know how to please yourself. When did *that* become the issue?

Actually, it's always been the issue. And you are probably better at making decisions than you realize. When, for example, was the last time you took your parents' advice on what TV show to watch or what to wear to school?

Because making these decisions is so easy, you may not be aware of the process behind them. Using it is almost automatic. But, by becoming *aware* of the steps involved, you can apply this process to decisions in almost every area of your life.

Let's take apart one of these easy decisions — what to wear to school, for example. The first thing you probably do is think about your image or what you would like your image to be. Your goal, then, is to dress in a way that will enhance this image. The logical next step is to consider your choices — the clothes you have or your budget for buying anything new. You can immediately rule out certain items, like the shirt Aunt Grace sent you from her last vacation, which, apparently, was to the planet Mars. And the boots you were wearing when you took that walk through the cow pasture at night.

Before you make your decision, you will also probably think about what *other people* wear — especially the people who fit your goal image. Finally, you evaluate your choices and consider which of your outfits comes closest to meeting your goal. And that's your decision.

Some decisions are harder to make, but the process is the same. On the following pages, you will learn a decision-making model that, with practice, can become as automatic as getting dressed in the morning.

Identifying Choices

Joyce decided she wanted to be a doctor the day her little sister was hit by a car. She saw how the staff at the emergency room calmly went about saving Sheila's life, as though they did this sort of thing every day. "Of course," Joyce thought later, "they do!" She couldn't imagine a more wonderful job.

She also wants to buy a car. There's no room for this in the family budget, so Joyce needs to come up with the money on her own. She could get a job at the local fast-food restaurant (it's about the only employer for teens in her town), but she worries about the effect on her grades. If they fall, she won't be able to get into the college she wants to attend. She also thinks that it might be a good idea to volunteer as a candy striper at the hospital in order to get some experience. But she clearly can't do this and hold down a paying job as well.

List Joyce's goals below.

1. _____

2. _____

Which would you say is her long-term goal? Which is her short-term goal?

It's important to differentiate between the two. Short-term goals are those things that seem essential to your happiness *right now*. Because achieving them can result in immediate gratification, it's tempting to focus on them. Long-term goals, after all, might take *years* to fulfill. Shouldn't you be allowed some happiness in the meantime?

Of course you should. And you will have it. But make sure it's not at the expense of your future. In 10 years, what will mean more to you — an impressive wardrobe or a rewarding career? An aging car or a comfortable income? If you consider your long-term goals first, decision making will become much easier.

What is Joyce's long-term goal? _____

What are the choices she must choose form now that will effect her long-term goal?.

1. _____

2. _____

3. _____

Gathering Information

Once you've determined what your choices are, you need to find out as much as you can about each option in order to make an *informed decision*. This is a term that usually refers to a decision based on facts and/or thought. The more information you have about your choices, the better your decision is likely to be.

Before Joyce decides to take a job in the fast-food restaurant, for example, she needs to find out:

1. How much the job would pay per hour
2. How many hours a week she could work
3. What the down payment and monthly payments would be on the kind of car she wants to buy
4. How much she would need to spend each month on insurance, maintenance, and gas for the car

Without this information, Joyce might decide to take the job only to find that she still can't afford to buy a car. Considering that she may have jeopardized her future by taking time away from her studies, this would have been a bad decision for Joyce.

Take another look at Joyce's choices:

1. To take a job in a fast-food restaurant
2. To volunteer as a candy striper at the hospital
3. To spend her time studying and maintaining her grades

Before she can choose the best alternative, she needs to know:

1. What grades she needs to get into the college of her choice
2. Which classes she must take in order to major in pre-med
3. The availability of and requirements for financial aid or scholarships at this college
4. How much she could expect to earn on the job

Can you list some other information that would be helpful to Joyce as she weighs her alternatives?

1. _____
2. _____
3. _____
4. _____

Evaluating Choices

When you've listed your alternatives and learned as much as you can about each of them, you are ready to evaluate your choices. A good way to do this is to list the pros and cons of each choice. You must also judge how likely each alternative is to be successful or get you what you want.

As you may have noticed, this process calls for a certain amount of guesswork. It is also possible to "load the deck" in favor of the choice you would *like* to think is most appropriate for you. It is in your best interest, however, to be as honest as you can while making your evaluations. This *is* the time, though, to consider your *feelings* about your choices. Taking into account the information you've gathered, does your intuition tell you that one course is most suitable for you now? (Many people are inclined to base decisions on their hunches *before* they've investigated the facts. If you're going to use your intuition, it's important to use it *in light of,* not *in spite of,* what you know.)

No matter how thorough and honest you are, though, it is not always clear which choice you should make. Each alternative will have its pros and cons. And there are no guarantees that any course you take will be successful. By keeping your goals and values firmly in mind, however, you can be confident of making good decisions most of the time.

Joyce began evaluating her choices on the chart below.

Identify your choices	Pros	Cons	Probability of success
Working at fast-food restaurant	Earn money to buy car	Not related to medicine — therefore no relevant experience	Since I am smart and reliable, I should be able to get this job
Volunteer at the hospital	First medical job for resume	Less study time — may lower grades	Since I am smart and reliable, I should be able to get this job
Not work at all	_____ _____	_____ _____	_____ _____

In the spaces remaining on the chart, evaluate Joyce's other choice — not to work at all so she can concentrate on her studies.

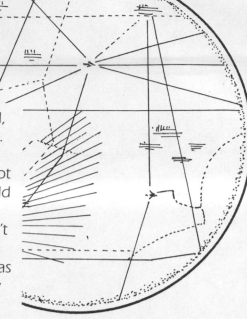

JESSICA'S STORY

Jessica needs to decide whether to take a math class next year and, if so, which one. She could take Algebra I, but she knows it's hard. Getting a good grade would mean less time for socializing with friends in the evening. Basic math would be easier. She always got A's and B's in grade school math, so it should be a cinch. She could even get by with no math class at all. She doesn't like math that much. But her counselor, Ms. Briscoe, reminded her that math isn't important for what it lets you become; it's important for what it keeps you from becoming. She said that, without math, Jessica was cutting her options for future careers by 75 percent. Did she really want to do that?

Use the chart below to identify Jessica's choices and evaluate each one.

Identify your choices	Pros	Cons	Probability of success
1. _____ _____	_____ _____	_____ _____	_____ _____
2. _____ _____	_____ _____	_____ _____	_____ _____
3. _____ _____	_____ _____	_____ _____	_____ _____
4. _____ _____	_____ _____	_____ _____	_____ _____

If you were Jessica, what would you do? _____

_____

_____

JOHN'S STORY

John is bored with school. He doesn't see how any of his classes relate to real life. Besides, he's probably going to fail English. Why not just drop out and go to work, he wonders. He's confident he could get a job in highway construction. He does enjoy the time he spends in the school's computer lab, however. The new computer with the graphic design software is especially intriguing. He's done some good work on it. He's heard of a vocational school program in this field. The school counselor told John that, if he brought his grades up, he could even get a degree from the local college in this field. Or maybe he should join the army. The recruiter promises John could get specialized training there.

Use the chart below to identify John's choices and evaluate each one.

Identify your choices	Pros	Cons	Probability of success
1. _____	_____	_____	_____
_____	_____	_____	_____
2. _____	_____	_____	_____
_____	_____	_____	_____
3. _____	_____	_____	_____
_____	_____	_____	_____
4. _____	_____	_____	_____
_____	_____	_____	_____

If you were John, what would you do? _____

_____

_____

The decision-making model you've just learned should work well in most instances. When you are making decisions about long-term goals, however, you will also want to take your resources, wants, and needs into consideration. This will let you see "the big picture" and should help motivate you to follow through with the actions that will help you achieve your goals.

The comprehensive decision-making model includes these steps:

1. **Define your goal.**
2. **State the decision to be made.**
3. **Analyze your resources.**
4. **Analyze your wants and needs.**
5. **Identify your choices.**
6. **Gather information.**
7. **Evaluate your choices.**
8. **Make your decision.**

Note: You've already done much of this work. See chapter 2, page 27 to analyze your resources. You analyzed your wants and needs in chapters 3-5. And in chapter 6, you identified your choices and gathered information on pages 150-155.

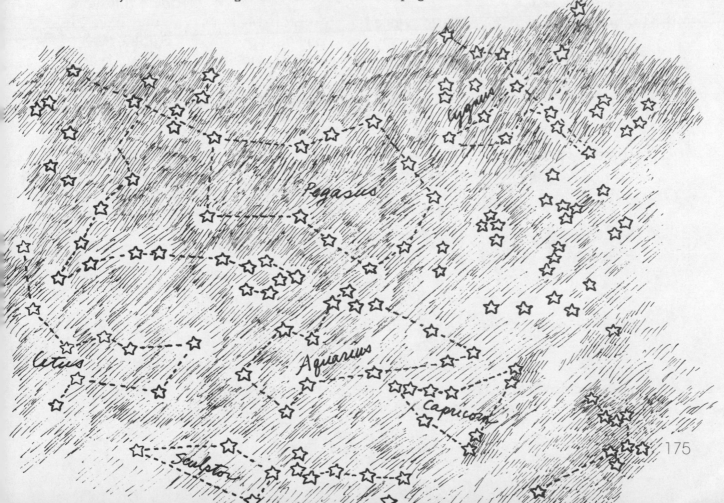

GLORIA'S CHART

Goal: Become a computer repair technician

Decision to be made: How and if to get the training I need.

Resources: Basic knowledge of computers

Good with hands

Like working with computers

Love detail work

Love to take things apart and put things together

Wants and needs: Value security — there will always be computers to repair

Want to work for myself someday to have flexibility for raising family

Want to be able to support family on one income if necessary

Identify your choices	Pros	Cons:	Probability of success
1. Go to trade school	— certifiable training, best guarantee of a job	— costs time and money	— should have no trouble getting into this program or doing this work
2. Learn on the job	— earn while I learn, use my skills	— probably low pay during training, no certificate, therefore lower pay in the long run	— may have to compete for opening, but can probably do the work
3. Become a waitress	— no training necessary, possibly higher immediate earnings	— not what I want to do forever, little security, doesn't make use of my skills	— should be able to get a job in this field

What choice would you make if you were Gloria? _____

_____

Gloria decided to take a two-year apprenticeship and save some of her earnings to get trade school certification at that point.

Complete the chart below for yourself. Identify and evaluate four possible career choices.

Goal: To identify a career that I will find satisfying.

Decision to be made: Which career would I find most satisfying.

My resources: _____

_____

_____

_____

My wants and needs: _____

_____

_____

_____

Identify your choices	Pros	Cons	Possibility of Success
1. _____	_____	_____	_____
_____	_____	_____	_____
2. _____	_____	_____	_____
_____	_____	_____	_____
3. _____	_____	_____	_____
_____	_____	_____	_____
4. _____	_____	_____	_____
_____	_____	_____	_____

Make a choice _____

How realistic is this choice? _____

Make a Decision

Making a decision is often difficult. But there's no way around it. You can stall and fret and change your mind. Sooner or later, though, *not* making a decision is making a choice. If you can't decide what to have for lunch, you are choosing not to eat. If you can't decide who to ask to the dance, you are choosing to go alone — or not to go at all. If you can't decide which college to attend, you are choosing not to attend college.

Decisions can — and often should — be changed. Many people fear making them because they think that no mistakes are permissible, that there's only one correct course of action. But people don't make decisions simply in order to be right. Executives, for example, are paid to make decisions so that work can proceed. They make the best decisions they can, but sometimes the decisions need to be changed. The point is, it's necessary to take action, and that's what making a decision allows you to do.

Basically, there are two styles of decision avoidance. Some people just can't bear to think about their choices at all and let things happen by default. This is a passive form of behavior. The other extreme is more aggressive. People with this behavior pattern suffer from "paralysis by analysis." They insist on examining every option and collecting every bit of information. But, afraid they may have overlooked something, they never quite get around to making a decision.

What is your decision-making (or avoiding) style? Check the place along the scale below that you think most represent your personality. If the words in the left-hand column describe your behavior, you may tend to avoid making decisions. If your behavior is better described by the words on the right, on the other hand, you may tend to make decisions too quickly. There is no right or wrong spot on the scale. But, by being aware of your tendencies, you may be better able to use them in your best interest.

passive	____ ____ ____ ____ ____ ____ ____	aggressive
contemplative	____ ____ ____ ____ ____ ____ ____	impulsive
controlled	____ ____ ____ ____ ____ ____ ____	free
rational	____ ____ ____ ____ ____ ____ ____	emotional
easily influenced	____ ____ ____ ____ ____ ____ ____	self-directed
delaying	____ ____ ____ ____ ____ ____ ____	expediting
cautious	____ ____ ____ ____ ____ ____ ____	risk-taking
structured	____ ____ ____ ____ ____ ____ ____	creative
agonizing	____ ____ ____ ____ ____ ____ ____	relaxed

By using the decision-making model — being as honest with yourself as possible — you may not always make the *best* decision. But you are probably not going to make the *worst* one, either. Letting others make your decisions, or making them by default, is giving up control of your life and your future. This is not the way to find satisfaction.

Evaluate your options, use your best judgment, take a deep breath, and make up your mind.

Keeping Your Options Open

It may seem that you are limiting your options when you make a decision. Sometimes you are. Deciding to quit school or to have a baby at age 16 can really put a crimp in your social life and your financial future.

Since making decisions is inevitable, however, keeping your options open is one more factor to consider when you make your plans. Should you take the classes you'll need to get into college even if you're not sure you want to go? Which decision would give you the most flexibility?

Remember that few decisions are irreversible or fatal. You *can* change your mind. And the better you get at making decisions, the better you'll be able to judge when it's time to make a change.

Flexibility is an important attribute. It shows every sign of being even more important in the future (more on this later). As the world changes, or as your own values, wants, and needs evolve, you will need to make adjustments — new decisions. With practice, you'll become secure in the knowledge that you've done it before and you can do it again.

You've made a decision. It's time to make your plans.

The rest of the book concerns HOW TO GET WHAT YOU WANT.

CHAPTER EIGHT

Setting Goals and Solving Problems

Skills for successful living

I always view problems as opportunities
in work clothes.
—Henry J. Kaiser

Efforts and courage are not enough
without purpose and direction.
—John F. Kennedy

Section Three:
HOW DO I GET IT?

Getting what you want differs from *deciding* what you want in one very important way: it requires action. It's easier to fantasize your future than it is to build it. But you must build it all the same. The remaining chapters in this book will teach you some processes that should be of help. *You* will need to come up with the energy, motivation, and confidence to get your plans off the ground, however.

HUBERT'S STORY

More than anything in the world, Hubert wanted to be appointed to the U.S. Air Force Academy. His father had attended the academy, and he said it was the best experience of his life. "It'll be even better for me," Hubert told himself, "I'll be a fighter pilot. I'll be a hero! Why not?" Hubert spent many hours in front of the mirror, trying on his father's old hat to see which angle was most flattering, and practicing the squint he was sure made him look like a young Clint Eastwood. "Or should I go for the Tom Cruise look?" Hubert mused.

Just one thing was standing in his way: Hubert's grades were well below the average he needed if he hoped to achieve his goal. But finding time to study seemed impossible. It was all he could do to finish reading the sports section of the newspaper before dinner. And, in the evenings, he had to hang out with his friends or maybe take a date to the movies. Plus there were all those great shows on TV. When Hubert's mother suggested he study on Saturday and Sunday afternoons, he was amazed. "Are you kidding?" he said. "During football season?"

Sometimes Hubert got discouraged. But it wasn't really his fault. Could he help it if his friends wanted to go out so much? Or if his teachers were less than understanding about his plight? He had nothing to do with setting up the admission standards, which, if you asked him, were totally unreasonable. There was always hope, though, Hubert insisted. Maybe the requirements would be lowered next year — at least for him. Surely when he explained, they'd see things his way. It was probably just a myth, that business about the military putting so much stock in following rules. So why worry? Everything would be fine, Hubert decided as he flicked on the TV.

Tools for Solving Problems

Whether he admits it or not, Hubert has a problem. And the prospects of his solving it are not good. If he doesn't change his ways, Hubert's life is likely to be plagued with unsolved problems.

Yours needn't be, however. Problem solving takes time and effort. It takes self-discipline, a quality with which Hubert is not well acquainted. But it can be done. In his book, *The Road Less Traveled,* author M. Scott Peck lists four techniques that, used together, should be helpful. Dr. Peck points out that using his techniques is not easy or painless. He says, in fact, that they will cause you a certain amount of suffering. But the pain is temporary, and it can lead to rewards that make it seem insignificant.

The first tool or technique, according to Dr. Peck, is **delaying gratification**. This means doing without the double fudge brownie you'd like to have now for the sake of the satisfaction you'll feel next month, when you've lost five pounds. For Hubert, making the effort to bring his grades up now would mean giving up time he'd like to spend with his friends or watching TV. But, if he gets into the Air Force Academy as a result, he might feel his sacrifices were worthwhile.

Delaying gratification is difficult because the rewards of living only for the moment are more tangible. You can *taste* that brownie. The pounds you thought you wanted to lose seem much more abstract, however. And, when temptation strikes, long-term goals can easily be forgotten or postponed.

As you learn to delay gratification — put off the temporary joys of today in favor of lasting rewards in the future — you will be acquiring an important tool in solving problems.

The second technique in Dr. Peck's problem-solving prescription is **accepting responsibility**. Hubert was willing to blame his friends, his teachers, even the TV programmers, for his bad grades. But passing the blame is not effective in solving problems. When the problem is yours, so is the responsibility to solve it.

This is a difficult fact to accept. Sometimes other people do things that upset you or disrupt your plans. If Hubert's friends didn't ask him to go out, for example, he might find it easier to get his studying done. But it is Hubert who wants to go to the Air Force Academy. And it is Hubert's responsibility to get the grades he needs to do that. His friends are his friends. They are not his keepers, counselors, or home room monitors. If Hubert could accept responsibility for his actions — and his problem — he would say no to his friends and struggle through his studies, which, in the long run, will help him achieve his goals.

The *good* news on this point is that taking responsibility also gives you the opportunity to choose. And, just as you are responsible for becoming the person *you* want to be, you are *not* responsible for becoming the person anyone else wants you to be. Pressure from home or from friends can be intimidating. It's natural to want to please the people you care about. But, if they want you to do something you feel is not truly you, not something you want to become, you can "just say no" with a clear conscience.

Dedication to truth or reality is the third problem-solving technique you need to master. Wishful thinking has not been shown to be nearly as effective. It *is* popular, however. That is why we see ads proclaiming that you can "lose weight painlessly overnight" or "make a million dollars at home in your spare time."

As long as Hubert clings to the belief that the regulations do not apply to him, he has no motivation to try to meet them. He should remember that the admissions committee is not privy to his daydreams. They have a procedure to follow, and they will apply it to him as well as to everyone else who wants to gain admission. "The truth isn't always pretty," as they say, but you cannot solve a problem by denying it exists.

Finally, problem solving requires **balancing**, which leads to *flexibility*. According to Dr. Peck, balancing is "the type of discipline required to discipline discipline." In other words, there are times when you *shouldn't* delay gratification. It's important to know how to live joyously in the moment — as long as you aren't being self-destructive by doing so.

And, even though it is important to recognize truth or reality, it is not always appropriate to act on that truth. You may be angry with a teacher who assigns too much homework on weekends, for example. But throwing a tantrum and stomping on your books is not going to change the situation or improve your standing in class.

In short, balancing requires judgment. Although you may be too young to always know the correct action to take in a given circumstance, you *can* learn to think things through before you act and make an honest effort to take the most effective or least destructive course.

"I must do something" will always solve more problems than "Something must be done."

—Anonymous

Crystal and Sterling were high school sweethearts who wanted to get married right after graduation. They didn't have any money, and they both wanted to go to college, but they didn't see why either of those facts should stand in the way. They were surprised and angered when Crystal's parents said the young couple would not be able to live with them. And Sterling's parents, even more unreasonably, said that if he and Crystal married, they wouldn't even pay his college tuition, as they had promised. "Alright then," said Sterling, "I guess I'll just have to get a job." Crystal, who was very good at math, quickly determined that, if Sterling earned the minimum wage (he was unlikely to find a better paying job) he would only make $8840 a year. That was clearly not enough to support the two of them, even if she did get an athletic scholarship, as she hoped.

Who is responsible for solving Crystal and Sterling's problem?

_____

If they get married right away, what sacrifices might they have to make?

_____

_____

If they wait and get married when they graduate from college what sacrifices will they

have to make? _____

_____

What facts should Crystal and Sterling consider before they make their decision?

_____

_____

What wishful thinking might come into play as they make their decision? How likely is

that to happen? _____

_____

If you were Sterling and Crystal, what would you do? _____

_____

185

Setting Goals and Objectives

Remember Marta's story, back on page 144?

After talking with her friend Jennifer, Marta decided she would like to know more about archaeology. Do archaeologists spend more of their time in the field or in the office? Who do they work for? How much education would she need? Where is most of the field work being done these days? Is it really hot there? Rainy? Would there be snakes?

These were all things she wanted to know before registering for the classes she would take next year. That gave her two months to do her research. Marta developed an action plan: she set her goal and then listed objectives for getting the information she needed.

Marta's action plan looked like this:

Goal: To answer my questions about archaeology by March 1.

Objective 1: Read at least one book or four articles on archaeology by January 20.

Objective 2: Interview Ms. Rogers in the science department by January 31 .

Objective 3A: Call City College and the Natural History Museum by January 31 to see if there are any archaeologists on staff.

Objective 3B: If so, interview a working archaeologist by February 14.

Objective 4: Research climate and reptile life at the three most appealing field sites by February 21.

Marta's action plan consists of setting goals and objectives. If she follows her plan, it is likely to get her the information she needs by the time she needs it.

Think of goals and objectives as a kind of recipe for getting what you want. The goal is the end product you want to achieve within a certain amount of time: let's say chocolate chip cookies (30 minutes). The objectives are the ingredients and the methods you use to make them. Once you know what the goal is (cookies), it's relatively easy to focus on the objectives (find the chips, never mind the onions).

Like ingredients, objectives are measurable (2 eggs, 3 cups of flour). And, like a recipe, they give you a time frame in which to work (bake for 12 minutes at 350 degrees).

The more specific your goals and objectives, the more helpful they will be. Consider the recipe once again. What if, instead of chocolate chip cookies, it was called "chewy, sweet things with brown parts inside"? Would you still have a pretty good idea of what you were making? Would you even be tempted to try? And, what if the recipe called for "a bunch of eggs" and "some sugar" and directed you to "bake until sometime in the future"? What are your chances of ending up with something even your little brother, the walking waste disposal, wouldn't eat?

Let's go over the definitions again, this time without the cookies.

A goal is a statement that specifies what you want to achieve or do within a certain amount of time. An objective is an action that will help you meet your goal — and measure your success. An objective tells you what will be different when you've accomplished it, by how much or how many, and by when.

Take a look at Marta's first objective:

To read at least one book or four articles on archaeology by January 20.

What will be different when Marta achieves this objective? We've underlined that part of her statement.

By how much or how many? The triangles point out the numbers.

By when? Notice the circled date.

Using these same symbols, go back to page 186 and diagram Marta's other objectives.

Now write and diagram some objectives of your own. Choose two goals from the following list and write three objectives for each.

To buy a new car in six months.

To save for a trip to _____ after graduation.

To make the _____ team next year.

To earn an A in _____ class.

To be accepted at _____ after graduation.
            (school)

Goal: _____

Objectives:

1. _____

2. _____

3. _____

Goal: _____

Objectives:

1. _____

2. _____

3. _____

Now write some goals and objectives of your own. Turn back to page 63. Choose three statements about your desired lifestyle. Write a goal and two objectives for each one. Think of three goals you can meet in the coming year that would help you achieve a more satisfying future. Write three objectives for each goal. Diagram the objectives to make sure they include all necessary components.

One of Maria's lifestyle goals was:

To have a career that is flexible enough to accommodate raising a family.

Her objectives:

1. Over the next two months, to interview five professional women who are successfully mixing career and family.

2. By the end of the semester, to research and identify eight careers that are flexible and yet offer the economic security required for a family.

3. By the end of the semester, to visit my counselor and make sure I am taking the necessary courses to prepare me for careers meeting my requirements.

Your lifestyle goal: _____

   Objective

   1. _____

   2. _____

   3. _____

Your lifestyle goal: _____

   Objective

   1. _____

   2. _____

   3. _____

Your lifestyle goal: _____

   Objective

   1. _____

   2. _____

   3. _____

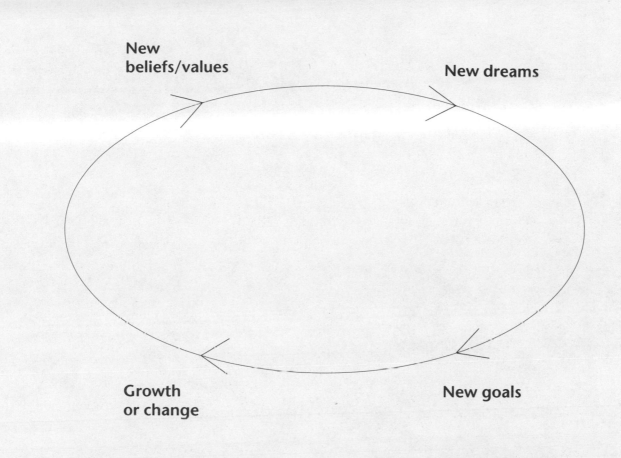

New beliefs/values

New dreams

Growth or change

New goals

Along with our careers, our lifestyles are determined largely by our values, opportunities, and desires — all things that tend to change over the course of a lifetime. When we set goals, we do so in an attempt to satisfy our present values. In reaching those goals, however, our minds are stretched, our limits are extended — and we change. We are constantly testing ourselves and our abilities. In the process we often find that we have found new values and set new goals, and so the process repeats itself. As our values change, our goals change. Reaching new goals leads to recognizing new values, and so on.

Keep in mind that life is an ever-changing and ever-growing process. The most satisfied people among us are those who actively set and reach new goals throughout their lives. If you can master this process, you are likely to have a rewarding future.

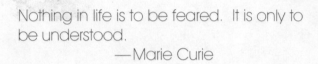

Nothing in life is to be feared. It is only to
be understood.
                    —Marie Curie

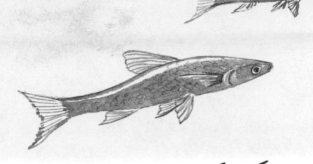

CHAPTER NINE

Avoiding Detours and Roadblocks

The road to success is dotted with many tempting parking places.

I have learned that success is to be measured not so much by the position that one has reached in life as by the obstacles which one has overcome while trying to succeed.
—Booker T. Washington

Section Three:
HOW DO I GET IT?

Many of the students at Carlos's high school were from wealthy families. Although Carlos's parents earned a comfortable living, they couldn't give him the cars or vacations his friends took for granted. They were proud when Carlos was accepted for admission at a well-known liberal arts college, but they told him he would have to help pay his own expenses. Carlos angrily told his parents that none of his friends had to do that. He wouldn't go to college at all if he had to work, too. It would be too hard. And, besides, it just wasn't fair.

No one in Liz's family had ever graduated from high school, much less gone to college. She'd always dreamed of becoming a teacher. But that wasn't realistic, she decided. What made her think she was any better than her family and friends? It woudn't be fair to leave them behind.

Karla liked to think about being an architect. But she knew she'd never be one. She didn't know any women who were architects. And, besides, she'd have to take all that math. It would be too hard.

Christy was one of many children in a poor family. He had cerebral palsy and didn't even begin to speak until he was 11 or 12. The only part of his body he could use was his left foot. He learned to type and paint with it, and eventually became recognized as both a writer and artist.

There are two important things you should know about life: it's not easy, and it isn't always fair.

The way you choose to respond to these facts will greatly affect your successes and life satisfaction. The first three stories are made up, but illustrate some common attitudes. The fourth story is true. Christy Brown was an Irish painter and writer. He accepted his illness as a challenge and set out to see what he could do with his life.

There are many people like Christy Brown, people whose attitudes take them far beyond what others would expect them to achieve. There are also many people like Carlos, Liz, and Karla, who let their attitudes limit their opportunities.

It's easy to find reasons to complain. It's easy to give up on a dream without trying harder to achieve it. But it's impossible to find satisfaction in a life that's based on negative feelings and behaviors.

Ironically, realizing that life is hard — for everyone — somehow makes it easier to overcome the obstacles and help you achieve your aspirations.

This chapter should help you recognize some of the most common detours and roadblocks to success so you can avoid them.

I Can't Do It Because . . .

I'd like to kiss you, but I just washed my hair.
—from an old Bette Davis movie

People can be extremely creative when thinking of excuses for not doing something. That's not surprising when the action to be avoided is undesirable. What is puzzling, though, is how often we make excuses for not doing the things we most want to do!

You may believe that your excuse is valid. But, somewhere, someone with the same problem or affliction is busy living your dream. Are you just going to sit there and let that happen? Why?

The responsibility of stating who you want to be and how you are going to get there can be very frightening. But not doing so is generally much worse, and can lead to a life of considerable dissatisfaction and unhappiness.

What's Your Excuse?

Ninety-nine percent of the failures come from people who have the habit of making excuses.
—George Washington Carver

We've listed some pretty convincing excuses below. Check any that apply to you.

- ☐ I'm a woman.
- ☐ I'm a man.
- ☐ I'm black.
- ☐ I'm white.
- ☐ I'm hispanic.
- ☐ I'm Asian.
- ☐ I come from a different culture.
- ☐ I'm rich.
- ☐ I'm poor.
- ☐ I'm too smart.
- ☐ I'm not smart enough
- ☐ I'm too ugly.
- ☐ I'm too fat.
- ☐ I'm too thin.
- ☐ I'm too short.
- ☐ I'm too tall.
- ☐ I'm blind.
- ☐ I have impaired vision.
- ☐ I'm deaf.
- ☐ I have a hearing loss.
- ☐ I can't speak.
- ☐ I have a speech impediment.
- ☐ I'm a paraplegic.
- ☐ I'm a quadraplegic.

- ☐ I've lost a limb.
- ☐ I have a debilitating disease.
- ☐ I've been treated for emotional problems.
- ☐ I've been persecuted for my beliefs.
- ☐ I've had a serious illness.
- ☐ I'm shy.
- ☐ I'm adopted.
- ☐ I'm an orphan.
- ☐ I come from a single-parent home.
- ☐ I've been abused.
- ☐ I've been in trouble with the law.
- ☐ I'm chemically dependent.
- ☐ I have to take care of a parent or sibling.
- ☐ I have a baby.
- ☐ My family won't let me.
- ☐ My family expects too much of me.
- ☐ No one believes in me.
- ☐ I can't do it because . . .
- ☐ Other _____

How valid are your excuses? Turn the page.

Somebody will always break your records. It's how you live that counts. The day you stop making excuses is the day you start to the top.

—O. J. Simpson

They Did It in Spite of . . .

. . . PHYSICAL LIABILITIES

Jim Abbott, a one-handed pitcher, won 12 baseball games in his rookie season with the California Angels.

Marlee Matlin, a deaf actress with limited speaking ability, won an Academy Award for her performance in *Children of a Lesser God*.

Stephen Hawking, Lucasian Professor of Mathematics at Cambridge University, considered the most brilliant theoretical physicist since Einstein, has ALS or Lou Gehrig's disease. He cannot walk or speak, but communicates through a computer attached to his wheelchair.

Winston Churchill, one of the greatest orators of the twentieth century, had a serious speech impediment.

Helen Keller, world-famous author and lecturer, was blind and deaf from birth.

Edgar Degas, a leading impressionist painter and sculptor, had extremely poor eyesight.

Actress **Patricia Neal** had to learn to speak all over again after suffering a serious stroke.

President **Franklin Roosevelt** had polio and was unable to walk.

Senator **Bob Kerre** of Nebraska lost a leg in Vietnam.

O. J. Simpson, crippled by rickets as a child, became one of the greatest running backs in the history of professional football.

Ludwig von Beethoven was totally deaf when he composed some of his greatest music.

John Milton, one of the greatest poets of all time, was blind.

Ray Charles and **Stevie Wonder** are two of many blind musicians.

Author **Alice Walker** and actor **Peter Falk** each have one glass eye.

David Stevens, a thalidomide baby born without legs, became a high school wrestling champion, a college football player, and a skilled baseball player as well.

Glenn Cunningham, who set a world record in the mile run, badly burned his legs as a youth. One leg was three inches shorter than the other, and the toes on his left foot were almost completely burned off.

DISCRIMINATION OR OPPRESSION . . .

Nelson Mandela remained the recognized leader of South African blacks despite spending more than 27 years as a political prisoner.

Vaclav Havel became president of Czechoslovakia only months after being released from a political prison.

Dith Pran escaped from a Khmer Rouge death camp in Cambodia and made his way to the United States, where he became a photographer for the *New York Times*.

Indira Gandhi of India and **Benazir Bhutto** of Pakistan became heads of state in two of the most male-dominated countries in the world.

There are now 180,000 female lawyers and judges in the United States, including Supreme Court Justice **Sandra Day O'Connor**.

There are 108,200 female doctors and 174,000 female engineers in the United States.

PERSONAL OR FAMILY PROBLEMS . . .

Eleanor Roosevelt, painfully shy, orphaned and considered unattractive, became not only first lady of the United States, but a writer, speaker, political leader, and one of the most admired women in the world.

Albert Einstein was considered mentally dull as a youth.

Abraham Lincoln suffered bouts of severe depression throughout his life.

Author, lecturer, and activist **Gloria Steinem** spent much of her childhood caring for her emotionally ill mother.

Rock guitarist **Eric Clapton** was abandoned by his mother as an infant.

Marilyn Monroe spent her childhood in a series of foster homes and orphanages.

Olympic Gold Medal winner **Greg Louganis's** dyslexia went unrecognized when he was a child. Because he was a stammerer, and a slow learner, his classmates called him retarded. He was also adopted.

Ten of the Forbes Four Hundred — the four hundred wealthiest people in the United States in 1989 — were high school dropouts.

Joseph Fernandez, chief of the New York City public school system, was a member of a street gang and a high school dropout.

Mary Groda-Lewis was an elementary school dropout, street fighter, and juvenile offender. She had a stroke while delivering a child and almost died, but she received a high school equivalency degree and went on to college. Determined to be a doctor, she was rejected by 15 medical schools before being accepted by Albany Medical College. She graduated from medical school in 1984, at age 35.

Romano Banuelos, the thirty-seventh treasurer of the United States, came to this country at age 16, when she was abandoned by her husband. She had seven dollars, two children, and no training. She did not speak English. Her first job was washing dishes, but with hard work and determination, she went on to become the manager of the largest Mexican wholesale food business in the world.

You can't change the circumstances of your birth, your family, or your past experiences, but, like many of the people on this chart, you can choose the way you let these things affect your life. You can concentrate on the things you cannot do. Many limitations are, after all, very real. Or you can make the best of the choices remaining to you. All of your opportunities lie in those areas that you *can* change, those places where you *can* act. Why waste energy on the rest? An old saying puts it well: "Lord, give me the strength to change those things I can, the serenity to accept what can't be changed, and the wisdom to know the difference."

Do you know of any people in your own community who have overcome handicaps or adversities in their lives? If so, add their names below. These people are all heroes. And they can be inspiring role models.

_____

_____

It takes courage to be who you really are. It also takes a lot of effort.

— Robert Shafer

Taking Responsibility

As you learned in chapter 8, *you* are responsible for directing your own life and solving your own problems. Trying to give that responsibility away (which is what you do when you make excuses) can get in the way of having the life you want. After all, if something isn't *your* problem, how can you solve it? But, since it isn't *anyone else's* problem either, it doesn't get solved. It becomes a roadblock to your success.

The way to remove the roadblock is to take responsibility for it. Once you do that, you can usually think of ways to get around it or move it out of the way. For example, if you can't speak French because it's *too hard,* there's not much hope of ever learning French. But, when you say instead that you can't learn French because *you haven't put in the effort*, a remedy comes readily to hand. If you can't go to college because your parents can't afford to send you, there's not much hope of going to college. But if you can't go to college because you're not willing to work your way through or seek out financial aid, a number of solutions seem possible.

Can you think of any excuses you've made recently that implied that something or someone else was responsible for your predicament? Write them below.

1. _____

2. _____

3. _____

Now analyze your own role in those situations and rewrite the statements, this time taking responsibility for the problem.

1. _____

2. _____

3. _____

200

STARTLING STATEMENT QUIZ

Circle the answer you think most accurately completes each of the following statements.

1. In 1984, _____ of the 9.2 million women aged 15-19 in the United States became pregnant.
   a. 250,000
   b. 500,000
   c. 1 million
   d. 1.5 million

2. About _____ percent of unmarried teen mothers keep their babies.
   a. 15
   b. 40
   c. 65
   d. 95

3. Out of every 10 teen mothers, _____ drop out of high school before graduation.
   a. 2
   b. 3
   c. 5
   d. 7

4. In 1987, _____ percent of families headed by a female, with children under 18 and no husband present, lived below the poverty line.
   a. 12
   b. 31.6
   c. 43.9
   d. 54.7

5. In March 1988, the overall unemployment rate was 6 percent. For high school drop-outs, the rate was _____ percent.
   a. 9.7
   b. 13.8
   c. 23.5
   d. 37.5

6. In March 1988, _____ percent of blacks who did not complete high school were unemployed.
   a. 9.7
   b. 13.8
   c. 23.5
   d. 37.5

7. One in every _____ teens aged 18 and above has not completed high school.
   a. 4
   b. 6
   c. 8
   d. 10

8. In 1987, the median income for full-time, year-round workers, 25 years and over, with four or more years of college, was $23,406 for women and $35,244 for men. The median income for workers with 1–3 years of high school was _____ for women and _____ for men.
   a. $15,897 and $18,777
   b. $12,940 and $21,269
   c. $9,927 and $14,903
   d. $16,461 and $25,394

9. The average life expectancy for alcoholics is _____ years.
   a. 37
   b. 45
   c. 58
   d. 72

10. _____ percent of teens who commit suicide are high on drugs or intoxicated on alcohol at the time.
   a. 10
   b. 16
   c. 31
   d. 47

11. The teenage drug problem in the United States is _____ in Japan.
   a. 5 times greater than
   b. 10 times greater than
   c. the same as
   d. 5 times less than

12. The percentage of students using drugs by the time they are sixth graders has _____ since 1975.
   a. tripled
   b. doubled
   c. remained the same
   d. declined

13. In a study of high school students who use cocaine, _____ percent said their grades had dropped significantly.
   a. 12
   b. 26
   c. 48
   d. 69

ANSWERS

1. c. There are about 1 million teen pregnancies each year in the United States.[1] For these young women, many life choices are significantly diminished.

2. d. Ninety-five percent, or almost all unmarried teens keep their babies.[2] A quarter million teen women are now heads of household. Most of them are poor.

3. c. Only half of the young women who give birth before age 18 complete high school, as compared with 96 percent of those who postpone pregnancy.[3]

4. d. Among female-headed households, 54.7 percent had earnings below the poverty line.[4] The poverty rate for all segments of the population at that time was 13.5 percent. In other words, female-headed households are about four times as likely to be poor.

5. c. The unemployment rate for high school dropouts was 23.5 percent, or almost four times the overall rate.[5] As society becomes increasingly dependent on technology, this figure may well go up significantly in future years.

6. d. The unemployment rate of blacks who did not complete high school was 37.5 percent.[6] One of the best ways to fight discrimination is to be well educated and trained for employment.

7. a. About a quarter of all 18- and 19-year-olds have not completed high school.[7] Programs are available in almost all communities to help these teens complete their education.

8. b. The median income for women who have not completed high school is $12,940, while for men it is $21,269.[8] Women, especially, need advanced education in order to earn a salary that will support a family adequately. Incidentally, women and men with less than eight years of education earn a median $9,927 and $14,903 each year, respectively. For high school graduates, the median income is $16,461 for women, $25,394 for men.

9. b. Alcoholics can expect to live only 45 years.[9] They are most likely to die from diseases related to physical deterioration, such as cirrhosis of the liver, ulcers, or heart disease.

10. c. Thirty-one percent of teens who commit suicide are high or intoxicated.[10] Suicide is the third leading cause of death among people 15 to 24 years old in the United States.

11. b. Our drug problem is 10 times greater than that of Japan.[11] In fact, the United States has the highest rate of teen drug use of any industrialized nation.

12. a. In the last 15 years, drug use by preteens has tripled![12] Today, one in six 13-year-olds has used marijuana.

13. d. Sixty-nine percent, or more than two-thirds of teens using cocaine have had their grades drop significantly.[13] The same study indicated that 30 percent of these teens were expelled from school. Refer back to answers 5, 6, and 8 to see how this could affect your future income. See answers 9 and 10 to see how it could affect your life.

Detours and Roadblocks

Your teen years are likely to be among the most difficult and demanding in your life. Your friends may push you to do things that aren't in your best interests. Your parents might pressure you to achieve at school or in extracurricular activities. Perhaps you have to hold down a job, as well. Dating can be worrisome. So can not dating. On top of everything else, this is the time you are supposed to make some of the decisions that will affect your entire future.

Sometimes it all seems too much. Why not just quit school or have a baby or start taking drugs? Wouldn't that relieve some of the pressure and pain?

Not for long. None of these behaviors can solve your problems. They can only delay their resolution. Short-term relief can lead to long-term regret.

Brad and Bart became friends in the second grade, when Bart's family moved in next door to Brad's. They were average students, but neither of them liked school very much. They had more fun in Brad's father's workshop, where they spent most of their summers taking things apart and putting them back together again. When Brad turned 16, he decided to quit school. It was boring and a waste of time, he said. Bart was tempted to join him, but he decided to stick it out. After graduation, he enrolled at the local vocational school and, within two years, was working as an electrician.

Who acted impulsively? In what way? _____

_____

Try to imagine what the future holds for Brad and Bart. Describe their lives 15 years later in the space below.

Brad's life: _____

_____

_____

Bart's life: _____

_____

_____

Josie and Juan went steady all through high school. So did Judy and Joe. During her senior year, Judy got pregnant and dropped out of school. She and Joe were married right after his graduation. Joe could not go to college to realize his dream — becoming a physical therapist — because he needed to work at a gas station to support his young family.

Josie and Juan were married after they graduated from college. Josie became a Certified Public Accountant, and Juan took a job as a high school teacher and coach.

Which couple acted impulsively? In what way? _____

_____

_____

What could life be like for these two couples in 15 years? Visualize their futures and describe them below.

Josie and Juan's life: _____

_____

_____

_____

_____

Judy and Joe's life: _____

_____

_____

_____

_____

_____

Sam and Janice started experimenting with drugs when they were in the tenth grade. By the next year, drugs had become the focus of their lives. Both dropped out of school. When Sam was hospitalized after an overdose, he decided to get help. He entered a community treatment program and began attending night school. With his high school degree, he was able to get into a two-year training program offered by a large hotel chain. Within five years, Sam was assistant manager of the hotel, proud of his profession and, most of all, proud of himself.

Janice never went back to school. Sam saw her once, waiting tables at the local diner. She looked tired, and when she explained she was divorced and supporting her three children on her income alone, Sam understood why.

Who acted impulsively? In what way? _____

_____

Describe what you think Sam and Janice's lives might be like 15 years from now.

Sam's life: _____

_____

_____

_____

_____

Janice's life: _____

_____

_____

_____

_____

Is It Worth Staying in School?

You decide. Go back to pages 150-151. What careers did you say you might like? List them below.

_____

Imagine that you quit school before graduation. Could you qualify for any of these jobs without a high school diploma?

Yes   **No**

If so, which ones? _____

If not, you need another plan. Review your personal information chart on page 27, your preferred lifestyle on page 63, your budget requirements on page 92 or your hardship budget on page 96, and your career portrait and priorities on page 134.

Now go through the career search process on pages 150-151 once more. This time, though, make sure that a high school diploma isn't required for the jobs you are investigating.

List three careers that meet your personal requirements but do not require a high school diploma below.

_____

Compare these jobs with the ones you listed at the top of the page. How are they different? Which careers do you think would be more satisfying? Why?

_____

_____

_____

Imagine your life 15 years from now. What do you think it would be like if you take a job from your second list, the one that doesn't require a high school education? Which would you find more satisfying — a career from the first or second list?

_____

_____

_____

The Economics of Bad Habits

Bad habits (smoking, drinking, drugs, and so on) will affect your physical and mental health and, thus, your ability to achieve. They are, therefore, another roadblock to success.

You have probably heard most of the common arguments for staying away from harmful substances. Most people usually hesitate to start a harmful habit because of the physical danger involved. But have you ever considered the economics of your habit? If you haven't taken up any of these habits, the following exercise might motivate you to stay away from them. If you already use a harmful substance, it might motivate you to put some energy into giving it up.

Complete the chart below, using the following information:

You are 18 years old when you begin smoking and you continue to smoke a pack a day for the rest of your life. If you live to be the national average age of 78 years old (your chances of reaching this age are lower because of your habit, by the way) and a pack of cigarettes continues to cost $1.80, how much will your habit cost every year? Every 10 years? How much over your lifetime? Can you think of any other ways you might like to spend this money?

	One pack/day	Other use for money
Cost/year	$	
Cost/10 years	$	
Cost/60 years	$	

You will spend $657 a year. That comes to $6,570 over 10 years, or $39,420.00 over 60 years.

Let's take our experiment one step further: If, between the ages of 18 and 65, you annually put $657 in a retirement account earning 10 percent interest, that account would be worth **$572,887** when you retire.

If you deposited your smoking money monthly instead of annually (*$54.75 per month = $657.00 divided by 12 months*), your account earning 10 percent interest would be worth **$701,851** when you turned 65.

In other words, if you saved the money you might have spent smoking, you would be able to retire with a guaranteed annual income (at 10 percent interest) of

> $57,288 per year if you made annual deposits, or

> $70,185 per year if you deposited your money monthly.

Some habits are much more expensive than cigarettes. Before you get involved with them, use the same equation to determine how much they would cost you over a lifetime.

Habit _____

Cost/day _____   Cost/week _____

		Other use for money
Cost/year	$	
Cost/10 years	$	
Cost/60 years	$	

If You've Decided to Give Up Your Dream

Evie always wanted to be a journalist. She did very well in college. Her teachers encouraged her plans. Then, two quarters before graduation, Evie quit college and married her high school sweetheart. She told everyone she'd changed her mind about journalism, that this was what she really wanted. Deep in her heart, though, she wasn't sure why she decided to give up her dream.

Keith wanted to be a social worker, but his parents always assumed he would take over the family business. He tried to talk with them about his plans, but they just didn't understand. The business they had worked so hard to build could not last without his help, they said. Keith decided he owed it to his family to obey their wishes.

Carlotta changed her mind about engineering when she took a look at the class requirements. How could she ever pass all those math tests? She might as well forget the whole idea, she told herself.

Sometimes there are good reasons to give up your dream. If your eye sight doesn't meet FAA standards, for example, you may as well forget about being a pilot. If the factory that has employed several generations of workers in your town closes its doors, you need an alternate plan. Or, if you come across an intriguing idea you hadn't thought of before, you owe it to yourself to give this new dream serious consideration.

Often, however, people give up too soon or for the wrong reasons. Usually, if they look more closely, these people find that they are acting out of fear.

Fear can take many forms. It can feel like obligation. It can feel like loss of interest. It can even feel like falling in love. Are you giving up on your dream because of fear? Consider the possibility carefully, especially if one or more of the following categories applies to you.

If You're a Woman

In a study of high school valedictorians, researchers at the University of Illinois found that, during their college careers, the young women in the group tended to scale back the ambitions they had on the day they graduated from high school.. It wasn't because of their grades. In fact, the females were getting consistently better grades than the males in the group. So why were they changing their plans while the males remained more dedicated to their goals? There are several possible answers.

Some women still think it's not "feminine" to be ambitious or successful at work. They are afraid that success on the job will take a heavy toll on their personal life — that they will not have the time or energy to marry or have children. This fear, however, is largely unfounded. Today, 68 percent of women with children under the age of 18 work for pay, and men are more and more likely to expect their wives to help support the family.

Women who plan to balance their careers with marriage and children may also believe that scaling back their plans for work will make them better mothers. In fact, though, women who prepare for the more demanding careers usually earn more and have more flexibility in their work lives — and these things help them be the kind of mother they want to be.

Let's explore this concept further. Do you think the workers in each of the careers below are mostly men or mostly women? First, in the space beside each job title, place an F if you believe more females work in this field, an M if you think more males do.

Now go back and circle the careers that would probably offer the most flexible hours. In other words, which workers could most easily decide to take time off in the afternoon to attend a son or daughter's basketball game? Some careers are decidedly more flexible than others.

_____ Child care worker	_____ Architect
_____ Receptionist	_____ Auto body painter
_____ Cashier	_____ Engineer
_____ Janitor	_____ Psychologist (PhD)
_____ Nurse (RN)	_____ Dentist
_____ Plumber	_____ Securities sales rep
_____ Elementary school teacher	_____ Chiropractor

Child care worker	$9,900		Architect	$30,900
Receptionist	$14,300		Auto body painter	$30,500
Cashier	$9,500		Engineer	$41,900
Janitor	$12,600		Psychologhist (PhD)	$40,100
Nurse (RN)	$22,500		Dentist	$64,800
Plumber	$22,700		Securities sales rep	$69,100
Elementary teacher	$24,900		Chiropractor	$64,800

Along the bottom of the following graph, first list the careers that are held mostly by women, beginning on the left-hand bottom column (we've already included the child care worker and receptionist as examples). Next add the jobs held mostly by men. Now, star the flexible careers, jobs in which workers can choose their own hours (we've used the chiropractor as an example).

$70,000

$65,000

$60,000

$55,000

$50,000

$45,000

$40,000

$35,000

$30,000

$25,000

$20,000

$15,000

$10,000

$5,000

Child care worker   Receptionist   *Chiropractor

Now use a pencil to chart the annual average salaries of the flexible careers. Use a pen to chart the annual average salaries of the nonflexible careers. (Note: The salaries we've used come from Department of Labor sources. Individuals might be able to earn a higher salary by working free-lance or starting their own small businesses.)

Suppose a woman with three children suddenly found herself the sole support of her family. Decide what a family this size in your community needs a year to live in minimal comfort.

$ _____ per year.

Now draw a double line across the chart at this dollar level.

Which careers from the list would be most suitable for parenting? That is, which would provide both flexibility and an adequate salary? List those careers below. (Hint: These careers are graphed in pencil, above the double line.)

_____

_____

Which of the careers on your list require either a college or vocational degree or some other type of special training? Circle them.

Do more men or women currently hold these jobs?

More men   More women

Role models are important, and women still have fewer of them than men. Consequently, it may be more difficult for young women to visualize themselves being successful as engineers, contractors, or whatever. As graduation draws near, panic may set in. It may suddenly seem more appealing to be a nurse rather than a doctor, an elementary teacher rather than an architect. But a sudden change in direction could be costly for your future family.

A note to young men: It's also to your benefit to encourage the young women in your life. When both partners in a household are capable of supporting the family financially, men have more freedom to enrich their own lives. For example, they might go back to school, or take time out to stay home with the children. They have more freedom to change careers, or to work at a job they love that doesn't support the family at the desired level. Or, if they are unable to work for any reason, they can rest assured that the family will be okay.

For more information on chosing a career that allows time for a family, see *MORE CHOICES: A Strategic Guide for Mixing Career and Family* (Advocacy Press).

IF YOU'RE "THE FIRST IN THE FAMILY" OR IF YOUR FAMILY DOES NOT SUPPORT YOUR DREAM

Some parents place a great deal of importance on education. Even if they did not graduate from high school or attend college themselves, they applaud the ambitions and abilities of their children. That makes things easier for the younger generation. In other families, parents may be quietly proud of their children. Or they may not see the point of further education. They might even think of school as a waste of time. In these situations, it is more difficult for sons and daughters to pursue their dreams. To do so might feel like betraying the family. But it is not disloyal to yourself. Although you may run the risk of losing their support, the true betrayal is to give up on yourself and your aspirations.

A similar — and perhaps even more difficult — problem arises when parents disapprove of your chosen career or have other plans for your future: you should be a doctor, not an artist; you should take over the family business instead of starting a flower shop. Your parents, of course, have reasons for thinking as they do. And you should listen to them respectfully. But, in the end, it is your life — and you are ultimately responsible for your life's satisfaction or dissatisfaction.

Without a doubt, it is easier to achieve your goals when you have the support of people you love and respect. If you cannot get that support at home, try to get it elsewhere. See pages 262-263 about locating mentors.

IF YOU DON'T THINK YOU DESERVE IT

No one can make you feel inferior without your consent.
—Eleanor Roosevelt

Remember the message center exercise on pages 50-53? What kinds of messages have you been getting about your future prospects? If any of them are negative ("You'll never amount to anything") or limiting ("remember your place"), you may have to fight periods of self-doubt and low self-esteem. At these times, it may seem like a good idea to give up and prove that the messengers are right: you are a failure and you don't deserve to succeed. A better idea is to acknowledge the messages, thank them for their input, and get on with your business.

Some people send *themselves* messages about their own worthiness. With so many poor, homeless, and starving people in the world, they reason, they have no right to pursue an economically rewarding career. Of course, it is important to be concerned about other people's needs. But, in fact, you can't solve many problems by becoming a victim yourself. Remember that, when you do achieve your goal, you will be in a better position to help others or to work for social change.

Can you think of a dream or ambition you had in the past that you have abandoned? Something you wanted to do or accomplish? Perhaps you dreamed of singing a solo in the school concert or asking your neighbor to the spring dance. Maybe, while watching "L.A. Law," you've dreamed of becoming a district attorney.

Think of a dream that you have given up or are considering giving up? (If you haven't given your dreams much thought, now is the time to start thinking about them seriously. Try to write them down when they come to mind.)

Before you decide to give up something you once thought you wanted badly, answer the following questions.

What was your old dream? _____

How long did you hold it? _____

When did you decide to give up your dream? _____

Why? _____

What is your new dream? _____

Why does it appeal to you now? _____

Is there hard evidence to support your decision to give up your dream (you can't carry a tune, you've flunked out of school, you've run out of money, and so on)?
_____

If so, is this just an obstacle, or have you really reached the end of the road?

_____

If there is no hard evidence, have you discussed your decision with your teachers or your adviser? What do they think?

_____

If you've come up against an obstacle, would you hang on to your dream if the obstacle would simply disappear (the math requirement is lifted, you win the sweepstakes)?

_____

If you've decided to give up your dream because of some rational obstacle (money, grades), think of as many possible ways to overcome your problem as you can. List them below. Are any of them workable?

_____

_____

If your reasons for giving up your dream are weak, your decision may be based on fear or anxiety. In the story above, for example, Carlotta decided not to become an engineer because she is anxious about math. She didn't fail at math. Her fear kept her from even trying to get through it.

Try not to let this happen to you. The truth is, everyone has anxieties. Trying to avoid situations that might make you feel uncomfortable can put unnecessary constraints on your life. The best thing to do is to learn how to tolerate the feelings that come with being ill at ease. If you can experience the anxiety (go to the party, get on the airplane), you will gradually overcome it.

By avoiding the thing that made her anxious, Carlotta deprived herself of that opportunity. What if she had signed up for a math class instead? Is there anything she could have done to lessen her anxiety?

She might have tried visualization. This is a technique that allows you to think about the thing you fear in great detail over a period of time. As you do this, you become less sensitive to the object of your fear and more confident about your abilities to deal with the situation.

If you, like Carlotta, suffer from math anxiety, try this exercise. Start by relaxing. It's important to feel at ease. Visualize yourself entering the classroom and taking a seat. See yourself listening to the lecture, and understanding what is being said. Allow yourself to experience your feelings when the first test is announced. Then think about a time when you were up against something you were sure you couldn't do but, with hard work and concentration, did successfully. Now see yourself studying for the test. Visualize taking your seat on exam day, picking up your pencil, reading the questions, and completing every problem.

If you repeat this exercise daily for several weeks, you should begin to feel more comfortable with the subject. When that happens, you will become more confident. That should help you perform better in the real class as well. (You can't just see yourself studying, however. You actually have to do it!)

Write a guided visualization that might help you conquer a fear you currently have. Try to see yourself actually doing whatever it is that makes you anxious and write the process below.

One Step at a Time

SALLY'S STORY

At first, Sally was delighted to be offered a full scholarship to a top-rated college. Then the anxiety set in: the college was way across the country, and she had never been away from home before. She'd never even been on an airplane (that was another fear). What if the other students didn't like her? After all, her family had no money or social standing, while many of her classmates would be wealthy socialites. She was tempted to turn down the scholarship. But she knew the education she could get there would help prepare her for law school and her dream — becoming a civil rights lawyer and perhaps, eventually, a Supreme Court justice.

Sally's school counselor, Mr.Chan, had a suggestion: "Why don't you make a list of five or six things that frighten you?" he said. Sally thought about the assignment overnight, then wrote down her concerns:

> Fear of flying
>
> Fear of living so far from home
>
> Fear of being an outsider because of my background
>
> Fear of public speaking
>
> Fear of confronting a friend who had betrayed a confidence
>
> Fear of failing my driver's test

"Okay," said Mr. Chan when she returned the next day. "Now rearrange your list. Put the item that concerns you least at the top and work your way down toward the situation that causes you the most anxiety."

That was easy enough, Sally decided:

> 1. Fear of confronting my friend
> 2. Fear of failing my driver's test
> 3. Fear of feeling like an outsider
> 4. Fear of public speaking
> 5. Fear of flying
> 6. Fear of living away from home

"Now what am I supposed to do?" she asked.

"Many people find they can overcome their fears by taking them on one at a time, from easiest to most difficult," said Mr. Chan. "So your job is to take care of the first item on your list as soon as possible. Then do the second, and so on.

"It's like a baby learning to walk. First you learn to creep, next you crawl, and then you stand up. Finally, you're ready to take the big step. But the earlier trials help you gain the skills and confidence you need to succeed."

That night, Sally couldn't get to sleep. How could she confront her friend? It made her head ache and her stomach queasy. She didn't like the feeling at all, but she did talk to Lynn the next morning. Afterwards, Sally was relieved — and very pleased with herself. She had done it! She'd faced her fear and kept her friendship intact as well!

Feeling more confident now, she made an appointment to take her driver's test two weeks later. She reviewed the manual, visualized passing the test, and got her mother to promise she'd practice driving with Sally for at least five hours before the exam. When Sally passed, she started to feel as though she could continue mastering her anxieties and gained a new sense of personal strength.

Next on her list, Sally had to learn that she could feel at ease with, and be accepted by, people from different backgrounds. She was invited to the mayor's reception for outstanding students, though she hadn't planned to go. Now, however, it seemed like a good opportunity. Sally decided to put aside her usual shyness and talk with everyone in the room. She felt self-conscious at first, but before long she was more comfortable and found herself behaving more confidently.

The next step, however, seemed more of a problem. For Sally, speaking with people one-on-one was quite different from addressing a crowd. Since this was a more difficult situation, she made another visit to Mr. Chan.

"Sometimes we have to break things down even further," he said. "These challenges can't be bridged all at once. It takes time to overcome them. I suggest you come up with a step-by-step plan that will lead you to speaking in public, say, within two months.

"Try visualizing yourself in the situation, thinking through the various steps. Practice this three times a day while you're relaxed until you are comfortable with the feeling."

Sally decided her first step would be to volunteer an answer in math class every day for a week. She practiced visualizing raising her hand and speaking until she felt ready to try it. It was uncomfortable the first day, but within a week it seemed more natural.

That gave her the courage to register for a speech class beginning the following month. Until it started, Sally kept volunteering answers in her other classes. At least once a day, she also visualized doing well in the speech class .

After the first day of speech class, when everyone had left the room, Sally went up on stage and stood behind the lectern. She pretended to adjust the microphone, and looked out over the auditorium. Her imaginary audience applauded her wildly.

Finally, the day came. Sally was well prepared for her speech. The class didn't respond as she had hoped but, when she thought things through, Sally decided she had done what she wanted to do. She could feel good about herself. And, the next time she got up to speak, the class did respond to her noticeable improvement.

By this time, Sally was beginning to get a sense of herself as a person who could achieve her other needs as long as she was willing to face and work through her discomfort. She began looking forward to her flight as one more in a series of heroic adventures — a challenge that she could conquer. She also began to feel she would be able to deal with the problems she would encounter in her new life at college. There would be times when she'd be homesick, she knew. And she would certainly be frightened or nervous about the many new situations coming her way. But she was learning she could tolerate discomfort and, if she faced it squarely, it would eventually diminish so she could get on with her goal: getting the best education she could and realizing her dream.

Like Sally, you may be facing a number of situations that make you uncomfortable or afraid. Some of them may even tempt you to give up your dream. List five or six fears you have or situations you are avoiding.

_____

_____

_____

_____

_____

Which of these do you think would be easiest for you to overcome? Which would be hardest? List again, starting with the situation that causes you the least anxiety and working toward the item that makes you feel most uncomfortable.

1. _____

2. _____

3. _____

4. _____

5. _____

6. _____

Think of a plan you could use to confront the first two items on your list. Write your

plan below. _____

_____

_____

_____

_____

Once you put your plans into action, record your feelings and experiences in the

space provided. _____

_____

_____

YORIK'S STORY

Yorik was born in Yerp, a tiny country on the Yorta Sea. Yerp is a beautiful place, and the Yerpese are generally a very happy people. Their main industry is raising yaks — woolly, horned cattle — for the production of yak yarn and yak yogart.

Yorik, unfortunately, is allergic to yaks and everything yakish. As such, his future in Yerp is limited. He is an ambitious young man, however, and decides that, if he is ever going to realize his dreams (and maybe even stop sneezing), he will have to leave Yerp. So, one day, he kisses his parents good-bye and gets on a boat to America.

Yorik arrives in the United States alone with little money. He doesn't know anyone here. He has little education, and just a limited knowledge of English. But he is healthy (at last!) and ambitious, determined to make a good life for himself. He thinks he should be able to accomplish his goals within 10 years.

What advice would you give Yorik? His career and lifestyle goal is listed below with a sample of his first year objectives. As Yorik's career counselor, write a 10-year plan that you think would help him achieve his goals. Include objectives for education or training, living arrangements, employment, and finances. (Do you remember the components of an objective? The diagrams we've used as an example should refresh your memory.)

Yorik's goal: At the end of 10 years, to speak English fluently, hold a satisfying job that I have trained for, own a home, and have $5,000 in savings.

Year one:

Education and training: To take English classes twice a week all year long.

Living arrangements: To rent a small, inexpensive apartment and, within two weeks, find two roommates.

Employment: Within 30 days, to find a full-time job I qualify for that pays at least $10 an hour.

Finances: To save $3,000 for education or training within two years.

222

Write your 10-year plan for Yorik:

Year one:

Education and training: _____

Living arrangements: _____

Employment: _____

Finances: _____

Year three:

Education and training: _____

Living arrangements: _____

Employment: _____

Finances: _____

Year five:

Education and training: _____

Living arrangements: _____

Employment: _____

Finances: _____

Year eight:

Education and training: _____

Living arrangements: _____

Employment: _____

Finances: _____

Year ten:

Education and training: _____

Living arrangements: _____

Employment: _____

Finances: _____

How did Yorik delay gratification in the plan you just described? _____

_____

How might he have acted impulsively? _____

_____

Did he take responsibility for himself?   Yes   No

What excuses might a less determined person have made? _____

_____

What anxieties might Yorik have had to overcome? _____

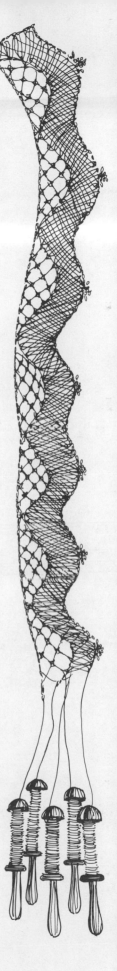

Taking Risks

Research shows that there are, basically, two different kinds of people when it comes to taking risks. Some people have a high need for achievement and are able to set and meet progressively more difficult goals. They see risk taking as a challenge and a learning experience. Others, afraid of failing, either take very small risks that teach them nothing or set their goals so high that no one could expect them to succeed. Their anxiety prevents them from growing and learning. Fortunately, since calculated risk taking is an important skill for successful living, it is possible to improve your ability to perform this task.

As a skill, risk taking combines the techniques for overcoming anxieties and making decisions. By definition, a risk involves uncertainty or danger. There is the possibility of losing something or suffering some kind of harm. It is reasonable, therefore, to be apprehensive. But taking a risk is also like making a decision. You choose to do it only when you have determined your goal, examined the alternatives, evaluated the pros and cons, and considered the probability of success. If, after going through that process, you decide the possible outcome is worth the risk, you need to trust in your ability to handle your fears and the discomfort they create — and go for it.

The inability to take calculated risks can be just as paralyzing as the inability to overcome fears. When you use the decision-making model, however, you will often find that the risk is a relatively small one. What is the worst thing that could happen if you ask someone for a date, for example? (Hint: It should *not* be the end of life on this planet. Nor should it brand you forever as a hopeless geek with a talent for self-deception. Try to evaluate which part of your anxiety is real and which part is not.) The worst that could happen is that the other person will decline your offer — and you will get on with your life.

Are you willing to take that chance? Perhaps not. It might be more important for you to hang on to the *dream* that he or she is harboring a secret passion for you than to actually have a date with this person. This is another point to keep in mind. Know what you are willing to risk or lose. Analyze the probability of the worst happening. If there seems to be a good possibility of losing something you hold dear, don't take the chance.

Here are some other points to consider about taking risks.

1. Don't try to solve *emotional* problems with *physical* risks. You can't solve the problems you have with your parents, for example, by driving carelessly, drinking or taking drugs, or risking pregnancy.

2. Make sure you take your *own* risks, not someone else's. And don't let anyone else take your risks for you. You will not be totally committed to a goal that is not your own. Nor can you expect someone else to feel as strongly about your goals as you do. In either case, the risk is likely to fail. (Example: A business is failing. Two people could possibly save it. Assuming they have comparable abilities, who do you think would be more successful, the person who owns the business, or the one who has no financial or emotional investment in it?)

3. Taking risks *does not* mean taking unnecessary chances. Young people, especially, are prone to taking hazardous risks in order to *prove themselves*. In truth, however, they prove little except their own lack of understanding. The only kind of risk worth taking is one that takes you a step closer to your stated goal.

4. Taking a risk is taking action. You cannot get to the place you want to be by simply wishing.

5. Do not take a risk unless you are willing to *make your best effort*. Commit yourself to your goal. As David Viscott says in his book, *Risking,* "If you don't intend to succeed, you intend to fail."

Getting Back on Track If You've Derailed

The advice on the preceding pages may be helpful if you are only thinking of giving up your dream, or if you've been temporarily sidetracked. But sometimes people get derailed and need more help than we can provide in these pages.

That doesn't mean their lives are hopeless, however, by any means. Reconsider the stories on pages 204-206, for example. Maybe Brad went back to night school to earn his high school diploma. Perhaps Judy did the same, and then she and Joe shared child care duties and worked part-time while going on to college or vocational school. Janice might have become an apprentice and learned a skilled craft that paid well enough for her to support her family more comfortably. All of them, though, would need guidance and assistance.

If you've quit school, if you're taking drugs, if you're pregnant or raising a child, or if you simply feel lost or abandoned, you may think your future is hopeless. It's not. But you must seek out the help you need to get back on track.

Can your parents help? They are probably just as worried as you are about your situation. But if you don't feel you can go to them, there are other resources.

People who know and care about you are often in the best position to give support, so consider talking with a favorite teacher or coach, a school counselor, your minister, priest, or rabbi, or another adult you trust and respect.

If you prefer to remain anonymous, consider calling local agencies such as the United Way, Alcoholics Anonymous, the Ys, Family Services, and Community Counseling Centers.

Whatever you do, don't do it alone. Get help! Yes, life is hard, but we're all in it together. There are people who want to help you. Let them. Get back on track. Use what you've learned and reaffirm your commitment to have the kind of life you want.

As Benjamin Franklin said, "Those things that hurt, instruct."

Hold fast to your dreams, for if dreams die, then life is like a broken winged bird that cannot fly.
—Langston Hughes

The most pathetic person in the world is someone who has sight but has no vision.
—Helen Keller

What is the difference between an obstacle and an opportunity? Our attitude toward it. Every opportunity has a difficulty, and every difficulty has an opportunity.
—J. Sidlow Baxter

Success or failure is caused more by mental attitude than by mental capacity.

—Sir Walter Scott

CHAPTER TEN

Attitude Is Everything

Learning to accentuate the positive

Think you can or think you can't, either
way you will be right.
—Henry Ford

Section Three:
HOW DO I GET IT?

The attitudes of success:
Self-confidence: "I can do it!"
Perseverance: "It can be done!"
Desire: "I'm going to do it!"

According to the old nutritionists' saying, "you are what you eat." But most people feel more like a hero or a failure or a nice guy than they do like a peanut butter sandwich. A more accurate saying might be, "you are what you think you are."

Attitude is everything. Muhammad Ali was telling the world that "I am the greatest" long before he became heavyweight boxing champion. In the movie *Funny Girl*, the Fanny Brice character played by Barbra Streisand sings "I'm the Greatest Star" *before* she becomes just that. During the worst days of the Great Depression, one of the most popular songs was "Happy Days Are Here Again." And soon they were.

It may seem unlikely, but it works: Telling yourself that you *are* the kind of person you want to become — acting as though you are that person *now* — helps you achieve your goals. Pretending is a way of practicing. And, without practice, how would we learn to do all the wonderful things we do?

The late actor Cary Grant once said, "I pretended to be somebody I wanted to be, and I finally became that person." In other words, pretending something is true can make it so. Perhaps this is not so surprising. If you want to become more confident, for example, *pretending* that you already are will probably lead to some kind of reward: getting the job or the date or the good grade on your speech. That experience will help *make* you more confident, which will help you keep up your act. As you continue to pile up rewards, you will do increasingly less acting. Soon, you may just find that you have *become a confident person.*

Another way to change your attitude is by using affirmations. Think back to the message center exercise on page 53. Affirmations are like the messages you get from other important people in your life. But they come from you — the most important person of all. You can tell yourself anything you like. Since the other messages reached you first, however, it will take time and constant repetition to replace them with new ones.

In order to be most effective, affirmations should also:

1. Be said aloud and repeated throughout the day, or written down. It's even more effective to record them on tape and listen to them while you're in a semihypnotic state such as running or lying down.

2. Include your name. "I, _____ , am a good student."

3. Be in the present tense. Say that the condition you hope to bring about is true **now!**

4. Be short, positive, and clear. "I, Waldo, am a graceful dancer" is better than "I, Waldo, am going to stop stepping on people's feet, tripping on my shoelaces, and running into the concession stand."

5. Be meaningful and believable to you!

What affirmations can you write about your future? In making your decision, consider reversing any negative messages from the exercise on page 52. For example, if your message from your father is "You can't do anything right," you might include an affirmation that states "I, Violeta, can do anything I set my mind to." If you've received the message "You'll never be good at math," you could benefit from an affirmation stating "I, LeeAnn, am a good math student."

We've included a few statements as examples. Use them if they could be helpful for you. Then write your own affirmations in the space below. Repeat them to yourself often. Act as if they are true now.

I, _____ , am confident when meeting new people.

I, _____ , am capable of getting a good job.

I, _____ , am good at making and keeping friends.

I, _____ , _____

I, _____ , _____

I, _____ , _____

The Six Es of Excellence

To excel means to do something of superior quality, to be the best that you can be — to know you've given your all to the task. By setting high standards and putting in an unusual amount of effort, an individual can go a long way toward assuring a quality existence.

Remember the formula for success from chapter 1:

$$\text{VISION} + \text{ENERGY} = \text{SUCCESS}$$

The formula for excellence takes this one step further:

HIGH STANDARDS + UNUSUAL EFFORTS = EXCELLENCE

This principle holds true in any line of work. By being the best cook or plumber or accountant in town, you can expect to live well. Better still, you can expect to be respected and to have a sense of personal satisfaction.

We want quality in the products and services we buy — even if we have to pay more for them. Doesn't it follow, then, that we should be just as concerned about excellence in the work we do and the way we live our lives? Satisfaction comes, ultimately, not simply from doing something, but from doing something well.

But excellence requires a conscious and ongoing commitment, a willingness to set high standards and exert unusual efforts. Not everyone is willing to sustain this kind of commitment.

How do you acquire excellence? For starters, you can apply the following principles to your life plans. It's not as hard as it sounds. The qualities seem to follow each other naturally if you start out with positive expectations. Take a look.

Note: Be patient with yourself. Mistakes are lessons, not proof that you can't make it. When matters look grim, be sure to recognize the positives.

EXPECTATIONS

The dictionary says that the word expectation "suggests anticipation of success or fulfillment." Actually, it's another word for vision. Expectations are often self-fulfilling prophecies — if you expect to be happy and successful, you have a good chance of achieving your goals. But, if you expect a poor outcome, that's about what you're likely to get.

Therefore it is important to have high expectations — for yourself and from yourself. Many people shortchange themselves by expecting only what they think is possible in a negative sense, or what others think they *should* want. Quite often, good students to whom learning comes easily believe that everything should be easy. When they come up against a task that requires effort on their part, such as learning to play a sport, they give up. They aren't used to making an effort to succeed so they limit their expectations to those things that they can do most easily.

What should you expect? Review your answers to the exercises in chapter 3. Expect to get what you said you want.

ENTHUSIASM

Once your expectations are in place, it's easier to generate the enthusiasm you need to accomplish your goals. Enthusiasm is the eagerness, interest, or excitement with which you approach a job or activity. It grows out of knowing what you want and doing what you love. If you have always dreamed of being a teacher, for example, your enthusiasm is likely to show up in your lectures and lesson plans. And you will probably be good at and happy in your job. If you really wanted to be a fire fighter, however, but went into teaching because that's what your parents wanted you to do, you aren't likely to have the same enthusiasm. You won't enjoy your job as much, and you won't do it as well as some others will.

This is the basic thesis of Marsha Sinetar's book, *Do What You Love, The Money Will Follow.* When you "discover your right livelihood," as she puts it, your enthusiasm will help assure that you give the job the time and attention it requires if you are to excel at it.

Of course, people don't always land their ideal job — at least, not right away. But if you can work up some enthusiasm for the work you do, you have a much better chance of moving beyond it to something more challenging and rewarding.

Author Brenda Ueland once said, "Never do anything you don't want to do." Few of us can follow that advice in all aspects of our lives, but it is something to keep in mind. Enthusiasm is the breath of life that can make even the most mundane tasks rewarding. When you plan your career, aim to do something you love, something you value. If you do that, your chances of excelling will increase because of your enthusiasm (love) for your project.

Nothing great was ever achieved without enthusiasm.
— Ralph Waldo Emerson

ENERGY

You can spend the rest of your life daydreaming about your future — or you can make your dreams happen. But it takes energy to put your plans into action. Fortunately, if you are enthused about what you are doing, the energy will usually come.

Everyone, though, has days when it's hard to get going. Of course, it's a good idea to take a day off now and again. But how do you overcome inertia when you know you need to get something done?

First try repeating your version of the statements on page 121: "I want _____ , therefore I should _____ ." If that doesn't work, try easing yourself into the chore. Promise yourself that if you do one small part of the project, or work on it for a short period of time (half an hour?), you can quit. Often, once you get going, the energy will start flowing, and you will be able to accomplish much more than you hoped. Finally, if all else fails, "just do it," as they say.

Of course, everyone has only so much energy. It's important to set your priorities and do the most important projects first. Otherwise they may not get done at all. There are many ways to waste time enjoyably. You should make time to do just that. But, generally, your life will be more productive and your free time more enjoyable if you do the things you must do first. That way, you can spend the remaining time any way you like, without worry.

Keep in mind, too, that energy springs from good health. Without adequate rest, nutrition, and exercise, it is difficult to maintain your energy level.

ENTERPRISE

By enterprise we mean the willingness to take calculated risks, the ability to recognize both problems and opportunities, and the creativity to make the best of either situation. The old saying, "When life gives you a lemon, make lemonade," was undoubtedly coined by an enterprising person.

This quality is probably the one most evident in "self-made" people, those who started with little and overcame adversity to become successful.

EFFICIENCY

An efficient person is organized. An efficient person gets things accomplished — on time. Efficiency is another aspect of taking control of your life. Without organization and planning, your life is manipulated by other people, or even by inanimate objects. You can prepare a super report, but if you can't find it when it's due, no one is going to give you the benefit of the doubt. Imagine how difficult it would be for an auto mechanic to repair a car if she couldn't find her tools. Or consider the absolute need for organization in an operating room.

Just as you are learning to plan your career and family life, you can learn to organize your closet, your desk, your files, your kitchen, your garage, and practically anything else. Books have been written on the subject. Seminars and classes are available. You can even hire someone to come in and teach you how to get organized and how to keep things under control.

ETHICS

Ethics is another word for your conscience, your sense of right and wrong. Some things are obviously wrong (embezzling funds from your employer, for example), but in other areas, principles are less clear. If you learn that your best friend cheated on an important test, should you report this fact to the teacher? Talk to your friend about your feelings? Do nothing?

Standing up for your beliefs or doing what you believe to be right isn't easy or efficient, but it may be necessary. Without integrity or moral courage, the success you attain may be hollow and have less meaning.

This is one area of life over which you should have complete control. No one can force you to betray your conscience.

Going For It . . . Work Is an Aggressive Act

In polite society, aggression is not acceptable behavior. At most parties, headlocks and half-nelsons are not appropriate forms of greeting. Those who attack the refreshment table in a flying wedge are unlikely to be invited back anytime soon. This will not come as news to most readers.

What *may* surprise you, though, is that aggression is *exactly* what it takes to succeed at work. Not aggression toward *people* (unless you happen to be a professional wrestler, a defensive lineman in the NFL, or the like), but aggression toward your work. Aggression takes many forms. It fuels competition as well as many other ways of behaving. Without some form of aggressive energy, we would probably never grow up.

How aggressive are you when you take on a job? Many people, especially women, find it difficult to identify with the term. It doesn't seem "nice" somehow. Wouldn't the world be a better place if everyone stifled their aggressive urges at work the same way they do at a party? Consider the following situations before you make up your mind.

SCENARIO 1
You are trapped in a burning house. The fire fighters arrive, but the doors are locked. Would you prefer to have them

a. wait patiently for a locksmith (the "nice" thing) or

b. kick in the doors and windows and get you *out* of there (extremely aggressive behavior)?

SCENARIO 2
You are unjustly accused of a crime. During your trial, your lawyer uncovers evidence that proves your accuser is lying. Should your lawyer

a. refuse to confront the witness because it wouldn't be polite or

b. nail him to the wall?

SCENARIO 3
Your car won't start. You need to be at an important conference in an hour. When you call the repair shop, would you rather have the mechanic

a. sympathize with your plight or

b. be at your house within 10 minutes and have you on your way in 15?

SCENARIO 4
You are a doctor. You witness a traffic accident in which a child is seriously injured. Should you

a. try to find out the name of the child's doctor and call him or her or

b. do what is necessary to save the child's life?

SCENARIO 5
You are one of five junior executives in a small corporation. Each of you is asked to write a proposal for increasing sales. Should you

a. be careful not to outdo your co-workers or

b. do your best, for your own sake and the company's?

SCENARIO 6
You are a newspaper reporter who hears a rumor that, if true, could drastically affect the lives of many of your readers. Should you

a. hope someone will call and tell you what's going on or

b. investigate vigorously to either verify the story or prove it's not true?

In his book, *Work and Love: the crucial balance,* Dr. Jay B. Rohrlich points out that "the basic aggressive urge . . . underlies all work." Perhaps that helps explain the language people use when they talk about what they do. They *tackle* problems, *wrestle* with alternatives, *make a killing* in the stock market, and so on.

According to Dr. Rohrlich, "'Perfection,' 'greatness,' 'mastery,' and 'excellence' revolve around the instinct of aggression." And, as the exercise above demonstrates, "people who fear and suppress their aggressive drives are usually unsuccessful at work."

The drive is there. Don't be afraid to use it. But try to recognize it and channel it consciously. Whether you are a poet or a fire fighter, remember that aggression, properly used, will allow you to do your best work. To quote Dr. Rohrlich once more, aggression "is a constructive, creative, and adaptive drive, the fundamental aim of which is to foster the survival, preservation, and enrichment of ourselves and our communities."

So go for it! It's your life!

You're the Boss

Picture yourself as an employer. Your restaurant, "Chris's Creative Cuisine," has been the center of your world since you started it 16 years ago. For the first three years, you worked 12 or more hours a day, taking charge of everything from setting tables to testing recipes. You saw little of your children, unless your spouse brought them by the restaurant. The personal costs were high — perhaps too high. The business finally became profitable five years after you opened. Now "Chris's" is one of the most popular dining spots in town. Things are looking good, and you are determined to stay successful. It's time for the annual performance review of your employees. What advice would you give to the following people if they worked for you?

SHARON

Sharon is a good waitress. She is late for work several times a week, but she always has a good excuse. She apologizes and says it won't happen again. But it does. Last week, Tim, another waiter, had to serve clients at Sharon's tables in addition to his own for two and a half hours because Sharon's car had broken down. (She says it's in good shape now.) Tim said he didn't mind the extra work, but it bothered you.

What is Sharon's problem? _____

_____

What advice would you give her during her evaluation?

_____

_____

Write and diagram an objective that Sharon might use to change her behavior.

_____

_____

JACKIE

Jackie, your pastry chef, has won several awards for her dessert, "Death by Chocolate." She has a tendency, though, to call in sick more often than seems likely. Even more unusual, her illnesses tend to occur on Saturday, your busiest day. Twice you've called her apartment to see how she's doing, but she wasn't home. When the mayor ate at Chris's last month, you were left with no desserts until Tim suggested an excellent bakery across town that delivers.

What is Jackie's problem? _____

What advice would you give her during her evaluation?

_____

_____

Write and diagram an objective that Jackie might use to change her behavior.

_____

_____

DOROTHY

Dorothy, your hostess, does a good job, but complains about other people's work a lot. She doesn't get along well with her fellow employees, and sometimes even lets her moodiness affect the way she treats customers. You recently overheard her make a rude remark to a long-time regular client and thought he'd never come back. Fortunately, though, Tim was able to make amends while he served dinner, and the client left smiling.

What is Dorothy's problem? _____

What advice would you give her during her evaluation?

_____

_____

Write and diagram an objective that Dorothy might use to change her behavior.

_____

_____

STUART

Stuart is a reliable waiter. He's never been late or missed a day of work. You've noticed, however, that since he started working for you, you've had to reorder things like candles and matchbooks more often than you did before. After a wedding reception at Chris's recently, you saw him walk off with the centerpiece from the bridal table. It's true that the flowers had been left, but Stuart didn't even ask. Tim had offered to deliver the flowers to patients at a nearby nursing home.

What is Stuart's problem?

_____

_____

_____

What advice would you give him during his evaluation?

_____

_____

_____

Write and diagram an objective that Stuart might use to change his behavior.

_____

_____

_____

_____

MAT

Mat is a busboy who would like to become a waiter. He does his job adequately — but no more than that. He usually has to be asked to refill water glasses or empty ashtrays. When a customer asked him for another basket of bread earlier tonight, Mat told him that wasn't his job. You can't help but remember the way Tim did the job when he started working for you.

What is Mat's problem?

_____

_____

_____

What advice would you give him during his evaluation?

_____

_____

_____

Write and diagram an objective that Mat might use to change his behavior.

_____

_____

_____

_____

240

Now that you've considered some less-than-perfect workers, can you describe a model employee? It might help to review the profiles above. If the characteristics described are undesirable, what opposite traits would make an employee valued by his or her employer?

Employee	Problem	Desired Behavior
Sharon	Tardiness	_____
Jackie	Untruthfulness	_____
Dorothy	Difficult personality	_____
Stuart	Dishonesty	_____
Mat	Laziness	_____

What characteristic did Tim display in each of the situations?

_____

_____

Describe the characteristics of people you would like to hire for your business.

_____

Chances are, your description is a fairly accurate definition of the term "work ethic." Being a good employee means being honest, on time, and so on. But the best employees — the ones who get ahead — display the traits that Tim does: they are creative, cooperative, and willing to do *more* than is expected of them. To many employers, a "good work habit" is more important in a prospective employee than knowing something about the job. They feel the job skills can always be learned. It's more difficult to instill the attitude they are seeking.

The work ethic *is* an attitude. The easiest way to acquire it is by liking what you do. Once again, it becomes apparent that, if you enjoy your work, you will do a good job And if you do a good job, you will succeed.

As some other people have said about work and success:

My grandfather once told me that there were two kinds of people: those who do the work and those who take the credit. He told me to try to be in the first group; there was much less competition.
— Indira Gandhi

The secret of success is to do the common things uncommonly well.
— John D. Rockefeller, Jr.

241

The Employee of the Twenty-first Century

It was a typical morning at the Millers. "Here's your juice, dear," Mrs. Miller said to her daughter, Angela. "Don't forget to take your cholesterol pill."

"I don't have time," Angela answered. "I'm late already, and I can't find my homework, my list of New Year's resolutions."

"I can't believe it's going to be 2015 in a few days," her mother said. "By the way, dear, you left the time machine on again last night. When your father came home, it was 1956 in here. You know how that always upsets him."

"Gee, I'm sorry, Mom. I was doing some research for my class in early television lit. I guess I just forgot to turn it off."

"I suppose you think you're the only one in the family who needs to travel in time," said her brother, Donald, as he came into the kitchen. "I was going to meet Herb and Joe in 1969 last night."

"Well, I certainly think my education is more important than your pleasure trips with your weird friends. Talk about a waste of time!"

"You see how selfish she is, Mom? I don't know why I can't have my own TM. Lots of other guys do. And I'm almost 16."

Like most stories about the future, the one above is almost certainly inaccurate. Chances are you won't have a personal time machine. You may never be beamed aboard the Starship Enterprise or travel back to the future in a souped-up Delorean.

But you will live there (in the future, that is — not in the Delorean). You will spend most of your working life in the twenty-first century. And, if you bring along certain attitudes, you might just "live long and prosper."

Although detailed predictions about life in the years ahead are unreliable, it is quite possible to make an educated guess about the general direction of events. Certain trends are already apparent and are becoming stronger.

Most of these trends are related to technology and the ways in which it has made our world smaller. Advancing technology, of course, is nothing new. But its speed is. Thousands of years elapsed between the invention of the wheel and the invention of the automobile. But the first successful airplane left the ground only two-thirds of a century before people landed on the moon. Back in the 1950s, the first commercial computers were called "electronic brains" and were so big they filled an entire room. Because of their expense, only a few of the very largest corporations could afford to use them. Today, computers are almost as common as TV sets. This paragraph is being written on a portable model that weighs only about six pounds.

Because of advances like these, business has taken on a global perspective. Businesses from around the world work together — or compete against each other — to produce quality products and services at affordable prices. In order to do this, they have changed. The people who work for them have had to change, too.

How well will you function in this new environment? The following self-evaluation quiz should give you some idea. Select the answer that best describes or comes closest to your feelings.

1. I view computers as:
   - ☐ a. an important tool.
   - ☐ b. a necessary evil.
   - ☐ c. . . .I don't want anything to do with them.

2. If I need to learn a new procedure while working on a computer, I:
   - ☐ a. get out my manual and figure out how to do it.
   - ☐ b. get help from someone who knows what to do.
   - ☐ c. give up — it takes too much time, and I didn't want to do it anyway.

3. I think of technology as:
   - ☐ a. something we all need to know and understand.
   - ☐ b. . . .I don't think about it much.
   - ☐ c. unnecessary — I don't need these new gadgets.

4. When I get my diploma at graduation, I'll probably think:
   - ☐ a. this is really just the beginning of my education.
   - ☐ b. about what I'm going to do now.
   - ☐ c. thank goodness, no more school.

5. When I have a question about something, I:
   - ☐ a. look up the answer or call someone who should know.
   - ☐ b. make a mental note to keep my eyes open for the answer.
   - ☐ c. forget about it — it probably wasn't important anyway.

6. I think of change:
   - ☐ a. as an opportunity.
   - ☐ b. with caution.
   - ☐ c. with resistance.

7. If, halfway through a project, it becomes apparent that my plan for completing it won't work, I would:
   - ☐ a. rethink my plan and come up with a better one.
   - ☐ b. worry about the project and hope to come up with a better plan someday.
   - ☐ c. lose interest and scrap the project.

8. When I'm around people from other cultures:
   - ☐ a. I appreciate their diversity.
   - ☐ b. I'm curious — but cautious.
   - ☐ c. . . .I am uncomfortable with people who are not like me.

9. The idea of traveling to other countries:
   - ☐ a. sounds exciting to me.
   - ☐ b. is of some interest to me.
   - ☐ c. does not interest me at all.

10. Learning at least one other language:
   - ☐ a. is important for everyone.
   - ☐ b. is probably a good idea.
   - ☐ c. is unnecessary — I can get by speaking only English.

To score your self-evaluation, go back and give yourself 3 points for every "a" answer you checked, 2 points for every "b" and 1 point for every "c". If your total score is 20–30, you have the attitudes that will make you a valued employee in the twenty-first century. They include the following.

[X] BEING COMFORTABLE WITH TECHNOLOGY

Today, people at all job levels — from the loading dock to the executive suite — use computers. Maybe you think you can't do it. But, a hundred years ago, people were probably saying the same thing about using the telephone. The new is always unfamiliar. That doesn't necessarily mean it is difficult. The best way to become comfortable with technology is to start using it.

[X] THE LIFE-LONG LOVE OF LEARNING

It's quite possible that some of the people who used to service those "electronic brains" are still of working age. What do you suppose they're doing now? Since they were obviously comfortable with change and technology, they are probably doing quite well. Perhaps they've had several different careers. Undoubtedly, they've learned a lot.

In a rapidly changing society, skills need to be updated frequently. There's always something new to learn. A love of learning will not only keep you employable, it will also enrich your life and make you feel a part of the advances that are going on around you.

[X] FLEXIBILITY

It's been said that, "nothing is certain but change." How well you deal with this fact will greatly affect your future success and happiness. It's one thing to be able to cope with change. Thriving on it is quite another. People who embrace change and can easily live with uncertainty are likely to be the leaders of tomorrow.

[X] AN INTERNATIONAL PERSPECTIVE

With Disneyland in Tokyo, McDonald's in Moscow, and Coke in Beijing, it's easy to see that the world is becoming a much smaller place. Businesses around the world are entering the global marketplace. Nations are joining together for mutual economic advantage. At the same time, people are celebrating their cultural diversity. They are also traveling more. Quite commonly, they are living and working away from their homeland. For those who can appreciate other cultures and speak at least two languages, the situation holds endless opportunity.

Do you need an attitude adjustment? If your evaluation shows that you could use improvement in any of these areas, make plans now to change. Write some objectives that will help you in the spaces below. (Turn to pages 186-189 if you need to review the process.)

Elliot's objectives are as follows:

Technology:

1. Take the advanced computer class next fall.
2. Subscribe to a computer magazine for the next year — and read it.

Love of learning:

1. Read two books on the publishing industry this summer.
2. Improve my tennis game by watching educational videos and asking Andre to coach me during the holiday break.

Flexibility:

1. Write three different endings for my short story and then choose the best one before handing it in.
2. Try to find a new summer job in a career I'm interested in learning more about instead of going back to work at the supermarket.

International perspective:

1. Join the Russian club at school this term.
2. Make three new friends from different backgrounds or cultures by the end of the school year.

Your objectives:

Technology:

1. _____

2. _____

Love of learning:

1. _____

2. _____

Flexibility:

1. _____

2. _____

International perspective:

1. _____

2. _____

A Final Note On Attitude

A reporter was interviewing a woman who worked for a famous actress. "What do you think about your employer's enormous success?" he asked as she transferred a load of the celebrity's clothes from washer to dryer. "I'm really pleased that she found something to fall back on," came the reply. "Because she doesn't know beans about doing laundry."

In his book, *Up from Slavery*, Booker T. Washington said, "there is as much dignity in tilling a field as in writing a poem." And that, finally, is what attitude is all about. It makes little difference what you do. If you can find pleasure in a job, if you do it well and with pride, any task becomes noble.

B. C. Forbes suggested that "whether we find pleasure in our work or whether we find it a bore depends entirely upon our mental attitude towards it, not upon the task itself."

The dictionary is the only place that success comes before work. Hard work is the price we must pay for success. I think you can accomplish almost anything if you're willing to pay the price.
—Vince Lombardi

If you love sleep, you will end in poverty. Stay awake, work hard, and there will be plenty to eat!
—Proverbs 20:13

The best-kept secret in America today is that people would rather work hard for someting they believe in than enjoy a pampered idleness.
—John W. Gardner

One thing you can learn by watching the clock is that it passes the time by keeping its hands busy.
—York Trade Compositor

When the grass looks greener on the other side of the fence, it may be that they take better care of it there.
—Cecil Selig

We are judged by what we finish, not by what we start.
—Anonymous

Some people quit working as soon as they find a job.
—Anonymous

There is no such thing as a big job. Any job, regardless of size, can be broken down into small jobs which, when done, complete the larger job.
—Walter P. Chrysler

The number of people who are unemployed isn't as great as the number who aren't working.
—Frank A. Clark

Belly dancing is the only profession
where the beginner starts in the middle.
—Anonymous

We learn by doing.
—Aristotle

CHAPTER ELEVEN

Getting Experience

Finding your first job

This chapter outlines the steps you need to take to get that first job in your field. The same principles apply to any job search. Learn them well. You will use them throughout your life.

There are many excellent publications with more detailed information on resumes, job hunting, applications, and interviews. Ask your teacher or librarian for suggestions if you need more assistance in these areas.

YOUR RESUME

A good way to start your job search is to write your resume. A resume (it rhymes with "yes, you may") is a summary of your abilities, education, and work experience. It introduces you to possible employers, who will use it to help decide whether you are qualified for a job. Writing it will help you define your talents and abilities, clarify your career aspirations, and present yourself well in job interviews.

A resume gives you an opportunity to present yourself in the best possible light. Everything you say must be true, of course, but you can include information that may not come out on an application form. If your resume makes you seem more creative, responsible, energetic, and so on than other job applicants, it may lead to an interview with the employer. That is its most important purpose: a resume won't get you a job, but it can give you the opportunity to meet the employer in person. Final decisions about whom to hire are usually made then.

A resume should be no more than one or two pages long. Appearance is important. Type it neatly. Better yet, if you have access to a computer, make copies of your resume on a laser printer. These look very professional. In addition, it is easy to change or update your resume whenever you need to if the original copy is stored on a computer disk.

Check your resume carefully to make sure there are no misspellings or typographical errors.

There are several acceptable resume styles, but the one most often used, and most appropriate for younger people, is the chronological resume. It should include the following parts:

1. **Your name, address, and phone number.** These should be clear, complete, and at the top of the page. Don't use abbreviations, titles (Mr., Ms.), or nicknames.

2. **Your job objective or goal.** Employers want to know what kind of work you are seeking. This statement will also help you decide what other information to include in your resume. As much as possible, the information in the resume should relate to your qualifications for the job you say you want.

3. **Your education.** If you are still in high school, list the school you are attending, along with the city and state, and note what grade you have completed. If you have attended other high schools, list them in reverse chronological order (start with the most recent school, and work your way back to the first one you attended). There is no need to list elementary or junior high schools.

If you have attended college or had other training beyond high school, list these schools, along with the years you attended and any degrees, certificates, or licenses you have earned.

If you have taken classes that relate to the job you want, list them as well. Include any skills learned or honors earned.

4. **Your work experience.** Include both paid and volunteer work in this category. Again, use reverse chronological order. Start with your current job, or the last one you held, and work your way back to your first job. Include the company name and the city and state in which it is located. Follow with your job title and the specific duties you performed on the job. Describe your duties with action words, such as "prepared," "delivered," and "collected."

5. **Your military service.** If you have served in the military, list the branch and dates of service. Include any duties related to the job you seek and any awards you received. If you were honorably discharged, say so.

6. **Your personal information.** Employers don't really care what your favorite TV show is (unless you're applying for a job on that set) or how many cats you have (unless you want to work in a pet shop). In other words, use this category for any information that is relevant to the job you seek. Your hobby of rebuilding small engines is definitely of interest if you are applying for a job as a mechanic's helper. But if you want a sales job at the boutique, it may not be worth mentioning. Turn back to page 27 and review your lists of strengths and skills. Some of these can be included here.

You might also want to include any character traits that relate to doing well on the job, such as "like a challenge," "always on time," or "never missed a deadline."

7. **Your references.** References are adults — not relatives — who can vouch for your honesty, responsiblitiy, and so on. Think of several people who would give you a good reference and *ask* if you may include their names on your resume. Consider teachers, coaches, friends of your parents, parents of your friends, your minister, priest, or rabbi. Provide their names, addresses, and home phone numbers. Do not give a business phone number unless you have permission.

Many people simply say "references available upon request" on their resume. This is perfectly acceptable, but you must still be prepared to provide the names if you are asked. So get permission and prepare your list even if you don't include it on your resume.

An example of a chronological resume is included below. Note again that, for this type of resume, education and work experience are listed *in reverse order*. That is, it starts by listing your most recent school or job and works backward to your first job or high school.

This resume is for a high school junior. Elena's long-term plan is to be a veterinarian.

```
Elena Lopez
1245 Calle Real
Los Angeles, CA 91000
(213) 555-1200


Objective: A part-time position feeding animals,
cleaning kennels, exercising dogs.

Education:  1988 — present Central High School.
Graduation scheduled for 1992.

Honors student.  Courses include biology, chemistry,
geometry, algebra, computer science.

Work Experience: 6/89—9/89 Retail salesperson
Bonnie's Boutique
Los Angeles, CA
Sold merchandise, created displays, unpacked and
arranged new merchandise, advised customers.

Pet Experience:  6/88—9/88 Pet tender
Cared for neighborhood pets while owners were on
vacation.  Responsible for daily feeding and
exercising.  Cleaned litter boxes.  Groomed
long-haired pets.

Personal: Hobbies include raising tropical fish and
breeding Siamese cats.

References: Available upon request.
```

Elena plans to send her resume to the local humane society as well as to boarding kennels, pet shops, and animal hospitals in her area. With it, she will include a cover letter, explaining why she wants the job. Although resumes are not directed to a specific person, cover letters should be. See the business letter format on page 159.

Use this page to write a draft of a resume for yourself.

Finding a Job

The next step in getting your entry-level job is deciding where you want to work. Your first instinct is probably to check the want ads for openings that meet your requirements and abilities. That's fine. But don't be disappointed if the job you're looking for isn't listed. Most people don't find their jobs in the classifieds. Fortunately, there are other approaches.

If you do find a position that sounds promising, by all means apply for it. Read the ad carefully and follow instructions. If it asks you to call for an appointment, do so. More likely, the ad will instruct you to write a letter of application and/or send your resume.

You already know about the resume. In your cover letter or letter of application, identify the position you are applying for ("I am writing to apply for the job of messenger advertised in the December 3 issue of the *Daily Bugle*"). Be sure to include all the information requested in the ad. Be as specific as you can about your ability to meet the employer's requirements.

Keep your letter short and neat, and send it to the designated address. Quite often, want ads are "blind." That is, they do not tell you the name of the employer, but ask you to send your letter or resume to a box number. This, of course, makes it impossible to tell whether the job location is right for your career investigation. Applying for these jobs is good practice, but don't count on getting your job this way.

Most experts agree that the best way to get a job is to decide where you want to work, and then apply for a job there. If you want to be a doctor and there's only one hospital in town, it's not too hard to figure out where you should be looking for work.

But sometimes it's not that easy. There may be dozens — or even hundreds — of law firms, restaurants, or clothing stores in your area. Here are a few ways to narrow down the field:

1. Consider the employer's reputation or your own feelings about the business. Where do you like to buy clothes? That might be a good place to start, especially if you've become familiar with some of the people who work there already. What restaurants are considered top-notch? Could there be a better place to learn?

2. Read the papers. Note which companies are making news in your chosen field. Follow up with more research at the library, if necessary.

3. Network. Ask other people if they know of a good company in your field. See if they know someone now working in the career you hope to have some day. Don't be shy. Ask parents, teachers, friends, relatives — anyone who might be able to help.

4. Or . . .

. . . Conduct an Informational Interview

This is an excellent way to learn more about your chosen career as well as to find a job. Here's how it works:

Get the name of someone working at the job you eventually hope to hold. A personal recommendation is best, but if you can't find anyone who knows someone in this field, try another route. Check the phone book or call the Chamber of Commerce. Professional organizations or unions may be able to help. Use your imagination.

Then call and ask for an appointment. It's okay. People do this all the time. Simply say something like "Hello, my name is Bob Johnson. My uncle Ted said you might be willing to talk with me about your job as a radio announcer. Could I take half an hour of your time to ask some questions?"

There are a few rules to follow: Be on time. Dress neatly. Be polite. Don't stay longer than you said you would. Send a thank you note afterward.

It is not appropriate to ask for a job during an informational interview. You can, however, explain your situation and ask your interview subject whether he or she can suggest some place where you might get the kind of experience you are seeking. You may get some leads. You might even be offered a job. Even if you aren't, you will have learned more about your prospective career.

Here are some questions you might use during your interview. Add some of your own if you like.

How long have you had this job?

What kind of education or training did you need?

> If you were still in school, would you do anything differently?

> What advice would you give me about preparing for this career? About working in this field?

> What parts of the job do you find most enjoyable?

> What do you like least about your job?

> Do you have any plans for a career switch?

> If so, what would you like to do?

Job Applications

When you've completed your research, you will finally be ready to apply for a job. In most cases, you will be asked to fill out an application form. Every employer has its own form, but most ask for the same kinds of information.

You will usually complete your job application at the employment site. Be prepared to do it right. Neatness counts. Read each question carefully and think about your response before you begin to write. Crossed-out answers give a bad impression. It's also a good idea to bring your own pen — one with a fine point that does not drip or smear.

You will need to have a social security number for any job you get in the United States. Do you have yours? If not, apply for your card now. Call or write the social security office in your city for information on how to do this. To locate the office, look under U.S. Government Offices in your phone book.

You might also need to have your birth certificate in order to prove your age. If you don't have this document, you can get a copy from the Department of Health in the state where you were born.

Some jobs might require a driver's license, as well. If you have one, bring it along. If you are under the legal working age in your state, you may also need to have a work permit. Ask your school counselor how to get one if you think you will need it.

Bring your resume along. Information on your education and work experience will certainly be needed. You might be asked to include your supervisor's name and phone number and your salary when listing previous employers. Be prepared to list your references, too.

Some forms ask for information you may not know offhand. Ask your parents for help if you don't remember any of the following:

Your mother's maiden (unmarried) name _____

Previous addresses if you've moved in recent years _____

Illnesses or health problems you've had _____

Dates of your last physical and/or vaccinations _____

Some other questions you should be prepared to answer include the following:

Do you have the legal right to work in the United States? (If you are a U.S. citizen or have a work visa, answer yes.)   Yes   No

How will you get to and from work? _____

When are you available to work (Days and hours)? _____

How may hours a week do you want to work? _____

What salary do you expect? _____

Have you served in the military?   Yes   No

Have you ever been convicted of a misdemeanor or felony?   Yes   No

Most forms ask you to sign and date your application before you turn it in to the employer. Your signature indicates that the information you have provided is true and complete. It also gives the employer the right to contact schools, former employers, or references to verify your answers.

The Job Interview

The personal interview is usually the final step in the job hunting process. The decision to hire you — or not to hire you — will probably be based on the impression you make here. Give yourself every opportunity to succeed by following these suggestions:

1. **Be on time.** An interviewer who's been kept waiting for 15 minutes will already have serious doubts about your work habits.

2. **Look good — but not flashy.** The interviewer's first impression of you will be based on your appearance. Hair should be clean, combed, and off your face. Clean and trim your nails, too. Appropriate clothing means ties and jackets for men, skirted suits or dresses for women. Take it easy on the jewelry and cologne.

3. **Look confident.** Sit up straight. Speak clearly. Make eye contact with the interviewer. Keep in mind that few people actually *feel* confident while being judged by a total stranger. The interviewer knows this and will make some allowances. But this is one of those situations where it helps to *pretend* you feel confident. With practice, you'll begin to feel more at ease.

4. **Be prepared.** You can expect to be asked a number of questions. Take time to plan your answers before the interview. If possible, practice with a friend, taking turns being the applicant and the interviewer. Better yet, if your school has video equipment, see if you can have your practice interview taped. That way you can see for yourself how to improve your presentation.

It's also a good idea to convince yourself that you want this job more than anything else in the world. The interviewer will pick up on your confidence and enthusiasm, and that can only help you. Be prepared, too, to tell the employer what you can do for the company, how you will be of value.

You might be asked some or all of the following questions. Write your answers here:

Why do you think you would be good at this job? _____

_____

How did you hear about this company? _____

Why do you want to work here? _____

_____

What classes are you taking in school? _____

_____

What is your favorite class? _____

What is your grade point average? _____

What are your strengths? _____

_____

What are your weaknesses? _____

_____

What are your hobbies? _____

What are your plans for the future? _____

_____

When would you be able to start working here? _____

How many hours a week could you work? _____

How would you get to and from work? _____

What salary would you need to earn? _____

Is there anything you'd like to ask me about the job? _____

_____

Dealing with Rejection

No one likes to be rejected. But, at one time or another, everyone gets turned away. This is especially true in the working world. There may be dozens, or even hundreds, of applicants for a single job. Since all except one will be rejected, your chances of being in the larger group are extremely good.

Your first response, of course, will be to take it personally. This self-blame can be on either the micro ("if only I'd parted my hair on the other side") or the macro level ("I'll never get a job if I live to be 150"). It's fine to review your performance so you can make improvements in the future. But the fact that you didn't get the job has nothing to do with your worth as a person. Nor does it doom you to a life of failure.

The best way to deal with rejection is to brush off your ego and try again. If you truly want to work at the firm that has rejected you, apply again. Employers respect persistence. Apply for other jobs, as well. When you are hired, you will find your sense of self-worth miraculously restored. If you give up, however, you will have to keep living with the idea that you failed. And you didn't. You just didn't try long enough.

Until you get that job, though, here are some things that might help you feel better:

Seek out and spend time with people who make you feel good about yourself. Stay away from those who are quick to find fault with you.

Do something you're good at. Playing the piano or shooting baskets or writing a poem can help you remember that you have many talents and are a capable person.

Improve your job hunting skills. Practice your interview style.

Watch your favorite inspirational movie — one where the hero or heroine overcomes unbearable tragedy or unspeakable evil (and you thought *you* had problems!) to become the champion or the star or save the world. If he or she can do it, so can you. As Rocky Balboa once said, "Go for it!"

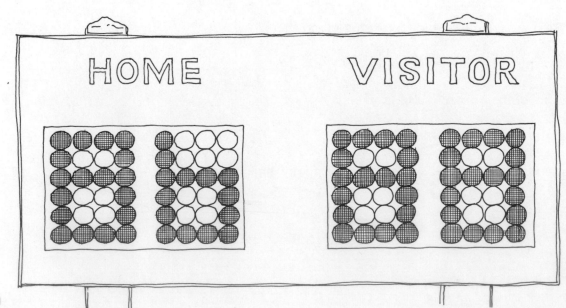

Accepting A Job

The day finally arrives — you are offered a job. What do you do now? Assuming that this is a job you *want,* there are still a few things to get straight. (If you have decided you *don't* want this job, thank the employer for the offer and explain that you have taken another position, you can't spare that much time away from your studies, or whatever. Don't burn any bridges, though. Don't say anything negative about the job or the employer. Even though you don't want to work there now, you might someday.)

Before you accept a job, make sure you clearly understand what it entails. What are your duties and responsibilities? When do you start? What days and hours will you work? Will you be expected to put in extra hours from time to time? Will you need a uniform? If so, where can you get one? Who will pay for it? How much will you earn, and how often will you be paid?

At higher levels, salaries are usually negotiable. Beginners, though, often must accept what they are offered if they want the job. Since the purpose of this job is to give you exposure to your chosen career, you probably won't want to make an issue of this.

However, if there is a salary range (say, from $3.65 an hour to $5.00 an hour) for people working at this job, you might practice your negotiating skills. Do you have any previous experience or special training that might entitle you to a salary at the higher end of the scale? If so, make your case. If you can't think of any reason why you should get the higher rate, it's best to accept the amount offered.

Making Connections

When you start working at your job, also start looking for mentors. One thing most successful people have in common is that, throughout their lives, they've had help from others. The word mentor means counselor or teacher. But employers or co-workers, parents, neighbors, coaches, and others can be mentors as well.

What do mentors do? Basically, they give you advice and encouragement. They "show you the ropes." If you've ever moved to a new school and found someone to tell you about different teachers and classes and advise you on what to wear, how to speak, and so forth, you've had a mentor.

Why are they important? For one thing, they save you time. Imagine how much longer it would take to learn the customs of a new school without advice: What is the one excuse you should *never* use with Ms. Bloom when your biology homework is late? What's the best thing to order in the cafeteria? Where do people go on Saturday night? When you go to work for a new company, a mentor can answer similar questions to help you feel comfortable and look competent.

Mentors are valuable sources of information. If they can't tell you what you need to know, they can often tell you where to look or who to ask. Because of their experience, they can teach you things you won't learn anywhere else. They can introduce you to other people in the company or in your field. They can help you become better known.

Best of all, mentors encourage you and push you to do your best. They applaud you when you do well. They build your confidence.

So where do you find them? Some people seem to know instinctively that they can benefit from these contacts, and have no problem recognizing potential mentors. Others haven't given the subject much thought. But it's not that difficult.

Teachers, coaches, and employers are the most obvious sources of help. Not surprisingly, the best way to get their attention is to do a good job. Teachers and coaches, especially, love their subject or sport and find great satisfaction in helping young people excel in their field. Similarly, employers are often more than willing to help promising employees learn their trade.

From time to time, you are likely to meet other people who could enrich your life. It's never a good idea — or proper behavior — to be a pest or to force your attentions on anyone. But most people are willing to answer a question or offer information. You can follow up with a thank you note. Perhaps a mentor relationship will develop. Perhaps not. Again, don't push it.

The best relationships develop naturally. If there's no friendship or rapport between two people, the association won't last.

We've talked about what a mentor can do for you. But what can you do for a mentor? Well, you can carry on in his or her tradition or trade. Better yet, you can continue the practice. As you establish yourself in your career, extend a hand to those who follow. Become a mentor yourself.

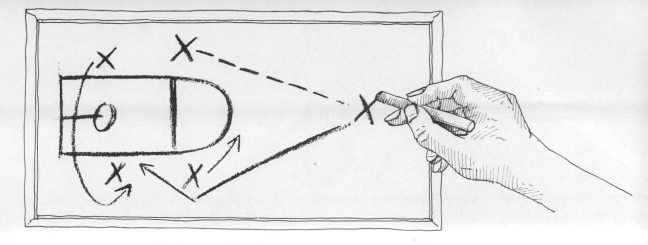

Can you think of people who have served as mentors for you in the past? List them below. What did they do that you found helpful?

_____

_____

_____

_____

How about now? Are there potential or actual mentors in your life? List them here. How have they, or how could they, help you?

_____

_____

_____

_____

Think about the training or work you are currently planning to get or do in the next 10 years. What kinds of mentors do you need? List them by title or classification below.

_____

_____

_____

_____

Have you ever been a mentor? To whom? What did you do? How did you feel about it?

_____

_____

_____

_____

Even if you're on the right track, you'll get
run over if you just sit there.
—Will Rogers

CHAPTER TWELVE

Where Do You Go from Here?

Writing your plan of action

A journey of a thousand leagues begins
with a single step.
— Lao-tzu

Section Three:
HOW DO I GET IT?

We know what we are, but know not what we may be.

— William Shakespeare
Hamlet

He that would eat the fruit must climb the tree.

As we said in chapter 1, success depends largely on two factors: vision and energy. By now, if you have completed the exercises in this book, you should have a better understanding of who you are and what you want; you should have a vision. You have also learned a number of skills and techniques to help realize that vision, a task that required no small amount of energy. But, truthfully, your work is just beginning.

In this final chapter, you will write your own plan. You will think about and list the actions you need to take over the coming years to achieve your goals. It may look like an overwhelming task. But do your best to complete it because "if you don't know where you're going, you're likely to end up someplace else."

Your plan should be a *flexible* guide, though. Unexpected problems and opportunities are sure to turn up, and you will need to adjust your plans accordingly.

Think of this chapter as a map. You know where you are. You know where you want to go. Your plan should serve as one route to your destination. You may decide to follow it all the way, or you may find an alternate path that suits you better. Perhaps you'll change your plans and head off in an entirely different direction.

That's fine. But make your decisions *consciously*. Have a *reason* for changing your mind. Then make a new plan, using this model if you like. Having a guide helps you remember your long-term goals and makes it easier to avoid actions that could keep you from reaching them.

Let's get started.

Sometimes, I think, the things we see
Are shadows of the things to be;
That what we plan we build . . . .
— Phoebe Cary
Dreams and Realities

Getting the Education or Training You Need

Education is a companion which no misfortune can depress, no crime can destroy, no enemy can alienate, no despotism can enslave. At home a friend, abroad an introduction, in solitude a solace, and in society an ornament. It chastens vice, it guides virtue, it gives, at once, grace and government to genius.
> —Joseph Addison

The things taught in schools and colleges are not an education, but the means of education.
> —Ralph Waldo Emerson

A whale ship was my Yale College and my Harvard.
> — Herman Melville
> *Moby Dick*

There are many ways to get the training and/or education you need. But most of them require one thing — **a high school diploma**. You also need a high school degree to be eligible for most kinds of employment. Without this ticket to opportunity, you are likely to end up with a low-paying, dead-end job — or no job at all. So stay in school. If you are having problems, talk with one of your teachers or counselors and arrange for special help. If you've already dropped out and can't go back to school, consult your local school district about adult education or other options. You might be able to earn a GED, or high school equivalency certificate.

After you have your diploma or certificate, you have a variety of choices:

COMMUNITY OR JUNIOR COLLEGES are two-year schools offering many advantages. They offer programs leading directly to employment. Credits may also be transferred to four-year schools. Usually, tuitions are low at community colleges, and, since there are so many of them (1,200), it's often possible to cut expenses even further by living at home. In addition, admission requirements are lower than at most four-year schools. So, if you didn't excel in high school, you have a chance to redeem yourself here. If you are interested in attending a particular school, write to it for more information. Or write to the American Association of Community and Junior Colleges (Suite 410, One Dupont Circle, N.W., Washington, D.C. 20036).

FOUR-YEAR COLLEGES AND UNIVERSITIES come in all sizes and varieties. Some are small liberal arts schools that usually stress a broad, general education. Other colleges specialize in certain kinds of training. State colleges and universities are usually large institutions that offer both liberal arts and more directed studies. Some four-year schools are very expensive and/or hard to get into. Others are quite accessible. To learn more about them, check the library for guides such as Peterson's *Guide to Four-Year Colleges*.

PUBLIC AND PRIVATE VOCATIONAL SCHOOLS offer specialized training in a wide variety of careers. Attending one of these schools for a year or two can lead to jobs paying as much or more than many of those requiring college degrees. Like junior colleges, public vo-tech schools usually offer low tuition and convenient locations.

APPRENTICESHIPS allow you to become a skilled worker through an arrangement between you and an employer, a union, and a school of some kind. According to the Department of Labor, more than 450 jobs can be mastered in this way. As an apprentice, you will spend part of your time on the job and part in the classroom. Usually, you will earn 40 to 60 percent of the normal job salary while you are learning. Contact the Department of Labor's Bureau of Apprenticeship and Training (BAT) for more information.

ON-THE-JOB TRAINING is available from many companies. It can take several different forms. You might receive instruction from fellow workers during and after work, you might be sent to classes elsewhere during the work week, or you might take classes on your own, with the company paying the tuition.

THE MILITARY offers both training for specific jobs and help with tuition once you are discharged. If you can get appointed to one of the military academies, you receive an excellent college education at no charge. (In return, you spend several years in the service after you graduate.) For more information, contact your local recruiters.

Ask your teacher, counselor, or librarian to help you find sources on any of these options. Extensive information is available. Before making your decision, you may also want to interview someone who has attended the school you are considering, or who has taken the path that appeals to you most (been an apprentice, served in the military, or whatever).

Where is it You Want to Go?

On page 177 you indicated which career you want to prepare for. Write that job title in the space below.

_____

How much education and/or training will you need to complete before you can get an entry-level job in this field (from pages 150-153)?

TRAINING   DURATION

_____   _____

_____   _____

_____   _____

_____   Total _____

Use the information above to determine how many more years of formal education or training you need. Enter that number below.

_____ years.

What educational requirements must you meet during each of those years (classes you need to take, grades you must maintain, and so forth)? List them on the following chart.

HIGH SCHOOL
This year:

_____   _____

_____   _____

Next year:

_____   _____

_____   _____

The year after:

_____   _____

_____   _____

And on . . .

_____   _____

_____   _____

POST-HIGH SCHOOL
Year one:

_____   _____

_____   _____

Year two:

_____   _____

_____   _____

Year three:

_____   _____

_____   _____

Year four:

_____   _____

_____   _____

Year five:

_____   _____

_____   _____

Year six:

_____   _____

_____   _____

Year seven:

_____   _____

_____   _____

And on . . .

Success generally depends upon knowing how long it takes to succeed.
— C. L . de Montesquieu

Nothing is so difficult but it may be won by industry.
—Terence

If you are planning to have a career that takes a great deal of education, the preceding exercise may have given you pause. Do you *really* want to spend that much time in school? Before you decide it's all too overwhelming, turn back to pages 114-119. Review the information there regarding the future dividends you can expect to earn for each year of education. Might it be worth the effort?

Remember, too, that although the investment of time may seem huge from your current perspective, you will earn the rewards over a lifetime.

Now that you have completed most of this book, rethink the following chart, paying particular attention to the next 10 years. How do they relate to the training and preparation you need to reach your career goal? Note that we have redesigned the chart to give you room to expand on your plans for the next 10-15 years. On each line write your major activity, type of education, or work for that year.

Now add what you think may be your major activities in your 30s, 40s, 50s, and so on.

How will the next 10 years of preparation impact the balance of your life?

90

80

70

60

50

45

40

35

30

29

28

27

26

25

24

23

22

21

20

19

18

17

16

15

10

0

Delaying Gratification

He that can have patience can have what he will.
—Benjamin Franklin

Who longest waits of all most surely wins.
—Helen Fiske Hunt Jackson

Waitings which ripen hopes are not delays.
—Edward Benlowes

Delay is hateful, but it gives wisdom.
—Publilius Syrus

Following a plan necessarily means delaying gratification. Turn to page 183 to review this concept. Admittedly, that's not always easy to do. It helps, though, if you are motivated and prepared. Answering the following questions should help you be both.

Can you think of sacrifices you might need to make in order to achieve your goal? Might you need to give up some social activities, for example? Will you have to spend some of the money you now use for clothes or recreation for tuition? List them below.

_____

_____

_____

_____

What commitments are you *willing to make*? (Will you study for a certain amount of time every day? Will you take a job to earn money for school?)

_____

_____

_____

_____

List the rewards you hope to gain from those commitments and sacrifices below.

_____

_____

_____

Do the rewards make the sacrifices and commitments seem worthwhile?

_____

_____

Turn back to page 121 and review the decision-making model on "the path of least resistance." Use it to complete the following statements.

Jodie's example: What do I want? *I want to be a lawyer.*

What are my choices right now? *To register for the advanced math class that will help me get into law school, or to take the art class that would be more fun.*

I want to *be a lawyer,* **therefore I will** *take the math class.*

What do I want? _____

What are my choices right now? _____

_____

_____

I want to _____ **therefore I will** _____

Facing Fears And Anxieties

Who feareth to suffer, suffereth already, because he feareth.
—Michel de Montaigne

He has not learned the lesson of life who does not every day surmount a fear.
—Ralph Waldo Emerson

My father, I remembered, had no fears at all. In that he differed greatly from me. But he could not be called a courageous man because he had no fears to overcome.
—Yael Dayan

One of the best ways to overcome anxiety is to anticipate it, face it squarely, and take personal responsibility for overcoming it. Remember that courage doesn't mean being *without* fear. It means acting *in spite* of fear. It's natural to be afraid or apprehensive at times. But don't let your fears get in the way of your goals.

In the space below, anticipate your fears by listing every excuse you can think of for giving up your dream.

_____

_____

_____

_____

Now list every reason or excuse you can think of for not successfully completing the preparation or training you need to have the career you want.

_____

_____

_____

_____

Now that you've faced your fears, take responsibility for them. For each excuse listed above, write an affirmation that counters the fear and gives you power. (See chapter 10.)

_____

_____

_____

_____

_____

_____

Experience shows that exceptions are as true as rules.
— Edith Ronald Mirrielees

What we suffer, what we endure, what we muff, what we kill, what we miss, what we are guilty of, is done by us, as individuals, in private.
—Louise Bogan

They are able because they think they are able.
— Virgil

Just as you are responsible for overcoming your own fears, you must take responsibility for solving your own problems. Can you think of any roadblocks or detours that might get in the way of your success during the next 10 years? (Review pages 203 – 215.) List those possibilities below.

1. _____
2. _____
3. _____
4. _____

Imagine your life 15 years from now. What will it be like if one of these events actually occurs?

_____
_____
_____
_____
_____

Remember that you are in control of the situation. Can you think of things you can do now to avoid these problems? Write a goal and two objectives that will help you do that in the space below.

GOAL: _____

Objective: _____

_____

Objective: _____

_____

Your Plan

On the following pages, you will write a detailed action plan for the next 10 years. Before you begin, sit down and visualize your life over this period of time. (See page 217 on visualizations.) How old will you be in 10 years? What do you think you'll look like? How do you want to feel about yourself and about your life?

Your plan takes into account your education and training, living arrangements, employment, and finances for each year. You already have a detailed plan for your **education**. Turn back to page 269 for that information.

Your **living arrangements** include both *where* you live and *who* you live with. Will you live with your parents? In a dorm or apartment? Will you live alone or with a roommate? Do you think you will be married in 10 years? Will you buy a house? Use your imagination.

Think about your probable **employment**. Will you be working for pay? Part-time or full-time? At what point will you begin working in your chosen career? Will you need to take jobs just for the money while you continue your education?

Whether you are employed or not, you will need money **(finances)**. Where will you get it? Will your parents support you? Will someone else? Do you think you might qualify for scholarships or financial aid? Or will you need to support yourself? How much money do you think you will need each year? Make an educated guess.

Your 10 Year Goal: _____

_____

Once you have a clear picture of where you'd like to go and how you might get there, write your plans below. Word them as measurable objectives if you can.

YEAR ONE — (Next year)

Education and training: _____

Living arrangements: _____

Employment: _____

Finances: _____

YEAR TWO

Education and training: _____

Living arrangements: _____

Employment: _____

Finances: _____

YEAR THREE

Education and training: _____

Living arrangements: _____

Employment: _____

Finances: _____

YEAR FOUR

Education and training: _____

Living arrangements: _____

Employment: _____

Finances: _____

YEAR FIVE

Education and training: _____

Living arrangements: _____

Employment: _____

Finances: _____

YEAR SIX

Education and training: _____

Living arrangements: _____

Employment: _____

Finances: _____

YEAR SEVEN

Education and training: _____

Living arrangements: _____

Employment: _____

Finances: _____

YEAR EIGHT

Education and training: _____

Living arrangements: _____

Employment: _____

Finances: _____

YEAR NINE

Education and training: _____

Living arrangements: _____

Employment: _____

Finances: _____

YEAR TEN

Education and training: _____

Living arrangements: _____

Employment: _____

Finances: _____

To get it right, be born with luck or else make it. *Never* give up. Get the knack of getting people to help you and also pitch in yourself.
— Ruth Gordon

You know, when you're young and curious, people love to teach you.
— Dede Allen

It's one thing to be responsible for your own actions, but quite another to feel you have to do everything on your own. Part of responsibility is knowing when to get help and where to get it. Review page 262 on the importance of mentors. Can you think of people in your life right now who could be of assistance in reaching your goals? If so, list them below. If not, start watching for these important people to turn up in your life. Whether or not you know any now, you are sure to meet others in the next few years. Learn to recognize them, and be open to the things they have to teach you.

_____

_____

_____

_____

In a world where there is so much to be done, I felt strongly impressed that there must be something for me to do.
— Dorothea Dix

If only I could so live and so serve the world that after me there should never again be birds in cages.
— Isak Dinesen

It is good to have an end to journey towards; but it is the journey that matters, in the end.
— Ursula K. LeGuin

I'm not one of those people who were born for nothing.
— Sylvia Ashton-Warner

Back on page 61 you stated your mission in life. Is it still the same? Restate or rewrite it below and refer to it often. Although your mission may change, it will keep you on course. In the end, you are likely to judge your own success or failure according to how well you have lived up to this purpose.

_____

_____

_____

_____

_____

What happens next is pretty much up to you. If you apply enough energy to your vision, there is no reason why you won't someday be able to say, as Samuel Johnson did more than two hundred years ago, "I knew very well what I was undertaking, and very well how to do it, and have done it very well." Good luck!

Some people see things as they are and say "Why?" I dream things that never were and say "Why not?"
— George Bernard Shaw

Hats off to the past; coats off to the future.
— American proverb

In the ordinary business of life, industry can do anything which genius can do, and very many things which it cannot.
— H. W. Beecher

Keep your eyes on the prize,
Hold on, hold on.
— Traditional civil rights song

We are a success: .
When we have lived well, laughed often and loved much. When we gain the respect of intelligent people, and the love of children. When we fill a niche and accomplish a task. When we leave the world better than we found it, whether by an improved idea, a perfect poem or a rescued soul. We are successful if we never lack appreciation of earth's beauty or fail to express it. If we look for the best in others, and give the best we have.
— Robert Louis Stevenson

INDEX

NOTES

1. Sheila B. Kamerman and Alfred J. Kahn, *Mother's Alone Strategies for A Time of Change* (Dover, Mass.: Auburn House Publishing Co. 1988), p. 115.

2. Ibid.

3. Claudia Wallis, "The Tragic Cost of Teen-age Pregnancy," *Time*, December 9, 1985.

4. U.S. Bureau of the Census, *Current Population Reports*, series P-60, no. 161.

5. U.S. Department of Labor, Bureau of Labor Statistics, Office of Employment and Unemployment Statistics, "Educational Attainment of Workers: March 1988."

6. Ibid.

7. U.S. Bureau of the Census, "School Enrollment — Social And economic Characteristics of Students, October", "Current Population Reports", Series P-20; and unpublished tabulations.

8. U.S. Department of Census, "Money Income of Families and Persons in the United States," various years, series P-60; and "Money Income and Poverty Status of Families and Persons in the United States," *Current Population Reports* 1987, series P-60, no. 161.

9. Drug Abuse Update, June 1986, Families in Action, American Medical News

10. Drug Abuse Update, June 1986, Families in Action, USA Today October 29, 1985.

11. Department of Education, William Bennett, 1987.

12. Ibid.

13. Calvin Chatlos, M.D., *Crack: What You Should Know about the Cocaine Epidemic* (The Putnam Publishing Group, 1986), p. 64.

ILLUSTRATIONS:

Itoko Maeno — 1, 2, 3, 4, 6-7, 8-9, 10-11, 12, 14, 18, 20-21, 22-23, 24-25, 26, 28, 30, 31, 32, 33, 36, 37, 38, 40, 42-43, 46, 47, 50-51, 52, 53, 54-55, 56, 58, 60, 64, 65, 69, 72-73, 74, 75, 76, 78, 85, 88, 90, 91, 92, 93, 96, 97, 98, 99, 103, 102, 104, 106, 110, 114-115, 119,122-123, 124-125, 126, 128, 130, 131, 132, 133, 134, 138, 140-141, 142-143, 144, 146, 147, 148, 149, 150, 156, 157, 158, 159, 161, 162, 164, 166-167, 168,-169, 174, 175, 176, 179, 180-181, 182, 185, 186, 187, 188, 189, 192-193, 194-195, 196, 200, 202, 203, 204, 205, 206, 208, 209, 210, 211, 213, 214, 215, 219, 223, 224-225, 228-229, 230, 232, 234, 235, 237, 238, 239, 241, 242, 245, 246-247, 248-249, 250, 252, 253, 255, 256, 258, 261, 264-265, 266, 268-269, 272, 275, 275, 276, 277, 278, 280, 281, 282, 283, 287.

Janice Blair — 67, 71, 80, 95, 100, 101, 112, 113, 120, 121, 135, 136-137, 170, 171, 173, 199, 222, 240, 260, 263, 267, 270.

Diana Lackner — 15-16, 44-45, 49, 62, 82-83, 87, 105, 107, 108, 109, 110, 183, 216, 218, 220, 285.

Some of the resources you might want to review as you make your career decisions are listed below.

What Color is Your Parachute? A Practical Manual for Job-Hunters & Career Changers, 1990 edition, by Richard Bolles, Ten Speed Press.

More Choices: A Strategic Planning Guide for Mixing Career and Family, by Mindy Bingham and Sandy Stryker, Advocacy Press.

The American Almanac of Jobs and Salaries, 1987–88, by John Wright, Avon Books.

Jobs! What They Are . . . Where They Are . . . What They Paid! by Robert O. Snelling and Anne M. Snelling, Fireside Books, Simon and Schuster.

Careers for Women without College Degrees, by Beatryce Nivens, McGraw-Hill Book Company.

Careers without College, by Jo Ann Russo, Betterway Publications, Inc.

College Majors and Careers: A Resource Guide for Effective Life Planning, by Paul Phifer, Garrett Park Press.

How to Start, Expand and Sell a Business, The Complete Guidebook for Entrepreneurs, by James C. Comiskey, Venture Perspectives Press.

The Road Less Traveled A New Psychology of Love, Traditional Values and Spiritual Growth by M. Scott Peck, M.D., A Touchstone Book, Simon and Schuster.

ACKNOWLEDGMENTS

We'd like to thank our peer reviewers for their important contributions to this work.

James C. Comiskey, Author and lecturer, *How to Start, Expand and Sell a Business* and *Successfully Self-Employed,* San Francisco, California.

Diana Frank, Community volunteer and philanthropist, homemaker and designer, Goleta, California.

Rochelle Friedman, Ed.D., Principal, Murray High School, Charlottesville, Virginia. Career Vocational Education Administrator, Albemarle County Schools.

Kenneth B. Hoyt, Ph.D., University Distinguished Professor, Kansas State University.

Susan A. Neufeldt, Ph.D., Clinical psychologist, Santa Barbara, California.

Laura Light, M.Ed., Reading specialist/language arts teacher, Murray High School, Charlottesville, Virginia.

Carl E. Lindros, M.B.A., President, Santa Barbara Securities.

Sarah Lykken, M.Ed., National Sales Manager, Carlson Learning Corporation, Minneapolis, Minnesota.

Also special thanks to:

Christine Nolt, book design and production; Pat Lewis, copyediting; Aptos Post, Inc., Linotronic Imagesetting; Janice Blair and Diana Lackner, illustration; Dick Rutan and Jeanna Yager for permission to use an image of the *Voyager* on the cover. And, to Deb Riestenberg, "thank you for sharing that."

MINDY BINGHAM

To date as author or co-author, Mindy Bingham's titles have sold nearly three-quarters of a million copies. They include the best-selling Choices: A Teen Woman's Journal for Self-awareness and Personal Planning and Challenges, the young man's version. Her children's picture books include the Ingram number one best-seller Minou; My Way Sally; the 1989 Ben Franklin Award winner; and Berta Benz and the Motorwagen. Mindy was the founder of Advocacy Press in Santa Barbara and was executive director of the Girls Club of Santa Barbara for 15 years.

SANDY STRYKER

Sandy Stryker is co-author of the best-selling Choices: A Teen Woman's Journal for Self-awareness and Personal Planning; Challenges: A Young Man's Journal for Self-awareness and personal Planning; Changes: A Woman's Journal for Self-awareness and Personal Planning; and More Choices: A Strategic Planning Guide for Mixing Career and Family. Her first children's book, Tonia the Tree, was the 1988 recipient of the merit Award from the Friends of American Writers. She is co-author of The World of Work Job Application File and has edited numerous other publications. A second children's book is currently in production.

ROBERT SHAFER

Making a courageous career change in midlife, Robert Shafer sold a very successful business, started over in college and today is a licensed Marriage, Family, Child Counselor with a clinical practice in Santa Barbara, California. The father of five, he has a master's degree in psychology and is a Ph.D. candidate.

ITOKO MAENO

Known for her sensitive and beautiful water colors Itoko's work has appeared in over 20 books. Born in Tokyo, where she received a bachelor's degree in graphic design, she has lived in the United States since 1982. Her refreshing style brings life to any text and offers the reader an oasis for contemplation.

Other books by Mindy Bingham and/or Sandy Stryker

Career Choices: A Guide for Teens and Young Adults: Who Am I? What Do I Want? How Do I Get It?, by Bingham and Stryker. Softcover, 288 pages. ISBN 0-878787-02-0. $19.95.

Instructor's and Counselor's Guide for Career Choices, Bingham, Stryker, Friedman, and Light. Softcover, 208 pages. ISBN 0-878787-04-7. $18.95.

Possibilities: A Supplemental Anthology for Career Choices, edited by Goode, Bingham, and Mickey. Softcover, 240 pages. ISBN 0-878787-05-5. $9.95.

Choices: A Teen Woman's Journal for Self-awareness and Personal Planning, Bingham, Edmondson, and Stryker. Softcover, 240 pages. ISBN 0911655-22-0. $16.95.

Challenges: A Young Man's Journal for Self-awareness and Personal Planning, by Bingham, Edmondson, and Stryker. Softcover, 240 pages. ISBN 0-911655- 24-7. $16.95.

More Choices: A Strategic Planning Guide for Mixing Career and Family, by Bingham and Stryker. Softcover, 240 pages. ISBN 0-911655-28-X. $16.95.

Changes: A Woman's Journal for Self-awareness and Personal Planning, by Bingham, Stryker, and Edmondson. Softcover, 240 pages. ISBN 0-911655-40-9. $16.95.

Instructor's Guide for Choices, Challenges, Changes and More Choices, by Edmondson, Bingham, Stryker, et al. Softcover, 272 pages. ISBN 0-911655-04-2. $14.95.

Mother Daughter Choices: A Handbook for the Coordinator, by Bingham, Quinn, and Sheehan. Softcover, 144 pages. ISBN 0-911655-44-1. $7.95.

Women Helping Girls With Choices: A Handbook For Community Service Organizations, by Bingham and Stryker. Softcover, 192 pages. ISBN 0-911655-00-X. $9.95.

Is There A Book Inside You? How to Successfully Author a book Alone or Through Collaboration, by Poynter and Bingham. Softcover, 236 pages. ISBN 0-915516-42-X. $14.95.

All of the following children's full-color picture books are 9" x 12", hardcover with dustjacket and illustrations by nationally acclaimed artist Itoko Maeno.

Minou, by Mindy Bingham, 64 pages. ISBN 0-911655-36-0. $14.95

Tonia the Tree, by Stryker, 32 pages. Winner of the 1989 Friends of American Writers Merit Award. ISBN 0-911655-27-1. $13.95.

My Way Sally, by Bingham, 48 pages. Winner of the 1989 Ben Franklin Award. ISBN 0-911655-27-1. $13.95.

Berta Benz and the Motorwagen, by Bingham, 48 pages. ISBN 0-911655-38-7. $14.95.

Mother Nature Nursery Rhymes, by Stryker and Bingham, 32 pages. ISBN 0-911655-01-8. $14.95.

You can find these books in better bookstores, or you may order them directly by sending a check for the amount listed plus $3.00 each for shipping to Able Publishing, 3463 State St. Suite 219A, Santa Barbara, CA 93105, (805) 967-9915 FAX (805)967-7741. Allow 3 to 4 weeks for delivery. For more information send for a catalog.

Write Able Publishing for more information on the *Personal Profile System* recommended on page 165.